EXPLORERS
— *and* —
EXPLORATION

VOLUME 9

POLAR EXPLORERS

Gavin Weightman

GROLIER
EDUCATIONAL

ABOUT THIS BOOK

The polar regions were among the last great unexplored areas of the world to yield up their secrets. The stories of the courageous people determined to conquer the desolate North and South Poles are great adventure stories. They are also a testament to the explorers' determination to overcome extremes of cold, ice, blizzard, deprivation, near starvation, and exhaustion to conquer the last unknown regions of the world. The achievements of legendary explorers such as Amundsen, Shackleton, and Scott not only make heroic tales but yielded valuable geographic and scientific data to extend our knowledge of the world we live in.

The book is divided into chapters, each one devoted to a particular group of expeditions. You can read the book from cover to cover, as a series of stories, or you can look in the index at the back of the book if you want to trace the exploits of one particular explorer—such as Roald Amundsen—who took part in more than one expedition. The index covers all 10 books of the set, so it can also help you to track earlier polar expeditions mentioned in this book which are covered in greater detail in earlier volumes. There are also lots of pictures and photographs to help bring the stories alive and specially drawn relief maps to show you the routes taken by the expeditions.

Published 1998 by Grolier Educational
Sherman Turnpike
Danbury, Connecticut 06816

Reprinted in 2001 and 2002

© 1998 Brown Partworks Ltd

Set ISBN: 0-7172-9135-9
Volume ISBN: 0-7172-9144-8

Cover picture: Tony Stone

For information address the publisher:
Grolier Educational, Sherman Turnpike, Danbury, Connecticut 06816

Library of Congress Cataloging-in-Publication Data
Grolier student library of explorers and exploration
p.cm.—Includes indexes.—Contents: vol.1. The earliest explorers—vol.2. The golden age of exploration—vol.3. Europe's imperial adventurers—vol.4. Scientists and explorers—vol.5. Latin America—vol.6. North America—vol.7. Australasia and Asia—vol.8. Africa and Arabia—vol.9. Polar explorers—vol.10. Space and underwater.

1. Discoveries in geography—Juvenile literature. 2. Explorers—Juvenile literature. [1. Discoveries in geography. 2. Explorers.] I. Grolier Educational Corporation.
G175.G75 1997   97-27683
910.9—dc.21   CIP
                                              AC

For Brown Partworks Ltd
Editor: Shona Grimbly
Designers: Joan Curtis and Paul Griffin
Picture research: Jenny Silkstone
Maps: David Heidenstam
Text Editor: Matthew Turner

Printed in Singapore

CONTENTS

Polar Explorers

Kim Westerkov/Tony Stone Images

THE MYSTERY OF THE ARCTIC

As recently as the late 19th century the bleak, icebound wastes of the Arctic remained impenetrable. Railroads now crisscrossed North America, and steamships chugged along great rivers into the interior of Africa and South America. But to the pioneers of the day, the great frozen seas and islands at the northernmost limits of the planet were almost as inaccessible as the Moon.

For centuries the hunters and whalers of North America, northern Europe, and Asia had pushed as far as they dared go into the Arctic Circle. There had been a long search for a fast sea route through from the Atlantic to the Pacific—the so-called Northwest Passage. The cost of the search for this elusive route had been huge in terms of lives and ships. One expedition after another failed, the bodies of those who died preserved on the white desert of the ice.

AN ALLURING MYTH

So in the late 1860s the great Arctic region was still largely uncharted. In fact a popular theory of the mid-19th century, put forward by the German scientist Dr.

Since early times, mariners had looked at the ice-laden waters of the North Atlantic (below) and wondered what lay beyond the horizon. Many centuries passed and many lives were lost before the mysteries of the Arctic Ocean were revealed in all their grim glory.

Hulton Getty

August Petermann, was that there was an area of sea near the North Pole that was ice-free and open because of the warming effects of the Gulf Stream. (This ocean current flows north from the Gulf of Mexico, parallel to the American coastline, and across the North Atlantic to northwestern Europe.)

> **It was widely believed in the mid-19th century that a warm, ice-free sea existed near the North Pole.**

At his own expense Petermann fitted out a small ship in order to prove his ideas. He put in charge Karl Koldewey, an experienced mariner, and the ship set forth in May 1868 in search of an open sea route across the polar region. Although the vessel returned unsuccessful in September, the venture did fire German enthusiasm for polar exploration.

A series of expeditions followed, one led by Koldewey and another by two Austrian army officers: Julius von Payer and Karl Weyprecht. The expeditions proved Petermann's open sea theory wrong, and they mapped out large tracts of Greenland. Von Payer also discovered a cluster of islands north of Russia, which he named Franz Josef Land in honor of the Austro-Hungarian emperor. He mistakenly believed these islands to be part of a large polar land mass.

THE SEARCH FOR FRANKLIN
One polar explorer whose achievements have sometimes been underestimated was the American Charles Hall. As a young man, Hall was fascinated by one of the big news stories of the day—the

Hulton Getty

Lieutenant Julius von Payer (above) and his men (top) discovered Franz Josef Land in 1873.

Hulton Getty

This drawing of Eskimos building an igloo was made by George Lyon of the British navy. With his companion William Parry, Lyon spent 10 months living among the Eskimos. His lively accounts of that period give us a fresh and fascinating insight into the lifestyle of these hardy people.

disappearance of the great Arctic expedition of John Franklin in 1845. Many explorers had gone in search of Franklin, and John Rae and Francis McClintock had found some relics of the party. But nothing conclusive was known and Hall was eager to go in search of Franklin himself. At last, in 1860, he received money from a wealthy financier and other donors, and hitched a ride on a whaling ship in May.

It was 15 years since Franklin had vanished, but Hall thought some of his party might have survived if they had adopted the Eskimo way of life. So he lived for two whole years among the natives of Baffin Island: he adopted their fur and skin clothing, lived in igloos, ate raw seal, and learned to travel with a sled and dog-team over the ice. It was

Hall who realized that the way to reach the North Pole and to explore the Arctic was by these proven methods. He argued that all explorers in the region should, as he put it, Esquimeaux-ize themselves.

On his first trip Hall found not a trace of Franklin's expedition. However, he found relics of Martin Frobisher's expedition which had explored the area in the 16th century. Hall returned to America with an Eskimo family, gave lectures, and set about raising more funds for another trip.

Now, however, the American Civil War was raging; Hall offered to command a Union ship but was rejected. In July 1864 he raised funds from whaling companies and newspapers and returned to the Arctic on another whaler. He lived there for five years among the Eskimo people, and it was they who told him the story of how the last of Franklin's party died of starvation, and showed him silver cutlery found alongside the frozen bodies.

Hall returned to America a hero. He was given government backing and the naval tug *Polaris*, and sailed in 1871 for the Arctic in order to discover, as he put it, "the northern axis of the great globe if possible, or the absolute proof of its inaccessibility." In this he failed, but with his great dog-handling skills and his Eskimo friends Hall pushed farther north than anybody before him—to latitude 82° 11' North. He also explored the east coast of Ellesmere Island, the remote land off Greenland's coast that was to provide a base for so many polar

Hall lived for two years among the Eskimos: he wore fur clothing, lived in igloos, and ate raw seal.

expeditions. Sadly, Hall died of heart failure during the trip, and the *Polaris* was wrecked on the return voyage. A few survivors drifted 1,300 miles (2,000 km) on ice floes to the coast of Labrador, where they were rescued.

A BRITISH EXPEDITION
In 1875, four years after Hall's death, a British Arctic expedition set out with two ships, the *Alert* and the *Discovery*. In command was George Nares; he had

When Charles Hall landed on Baffin Island (below) in 1860, he was looking for Sir John Franklin—but instead found relics of Martin Frobisher's voyages made in the 1570s.

Kennan Ward/Corbis

Hulton Getty

The British expedition of 1875 led by George Nares (above, with his crew) suffered terribly in the Arctic. Several men lost their fingers and toes to frostbite, and many of the party were driven to eating handfuls of snow, so great was their thirst.

been second in command on the *Resolute*, which had gone in search of Franklin in 1852–1854, and he had more recently sailed the world in a steamship studying the oceans. Although Nares had no Arctic experience, he was a skilled sailor, and piloted the ships through icy seas up the west coast of Greenland, to the edge of the frozen Arctic Ocean itself.

From the coast Nares's team set off on foot, taking only a few dogs and some fresh musk-ox meat. Foolishly, they did not use the Eskimo survival techniques that Hall had learned so patiently. They hauled their own sleds, and the first party bound for the Pole got as far as the north of Ellesmere Island. But they

suffered from exhaustion and scurvy (due to a lack of fresh food) and had to turn back. A second party got a mile closer to the Pole than any previous explorer, and the following summer a third party broke that record by 48 miles (77 km), despite terrible outbreaks of scurvy.

This was the last of the traditional British naval assaults on the Arctic, and though it was poorly organized, it represented a great achievement. Both ships returned safely in 1876, and Nares established some key facts. Greenland was proved to be an island and not a peninsula attached to the ice cap. Nares also confirmed most of Charles Hall's mapping of the region and collected

ESKIMO OR INUIT?

The native inhabitants of Arctic regions include members of several different races, tribes, and cultures, each with their own language or subtly unique dialect. Since the 16th century, however, the native peoples from eastern Siberia east to Labrador and Greenland have been referred to under the general term of Eskimo.

Nowadays, the native peoples of Canada and Greenland prefer to call themselves Inuit—a word from one of their languages meaning "the people." Those in Alaska, however, still describe themselves as Eskimo.

information about the ice. Perhaps most importantly, he guessed—correctly—that the Arctic Ocean could provide no open routes across the pole: that at its bitterly cold heart lay a permanently frozen sea.

THE NORTHEAST PASSAGE

The mapping of the southwestern regions of the Arctic Circle was taking shape. Explorers from Sweden, where there was a great tradition of exploration, had played a key role in this. Among them was Baron Nils Nordenskjöld, who made his first Arctic foray to Spitsbergen in 1858. Over the following two decades Nordenskjöld explored Greenland and even made an attempt on the North Pole with teams of reindeer drawing sleds.

As a scientist, Nordenskjöld made many valuable observations. His great

George Nares set out to the Arctic in the Alert *(below)* and Discovery *in an attempt to reach the North Pole. The expedition succeeded in getting nearer to the pole than any earlier explorer, but they were defeated by sheets of ice and had to turn back.*

Hulton Getty

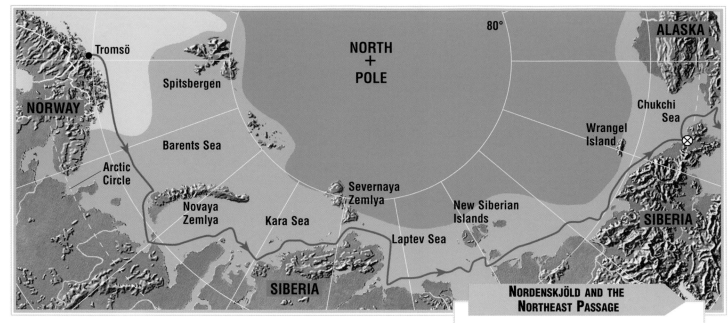

NORDENSKJÖLD AND THE
NORTHEAST PASSAGE

Nordenskjöld's route
(1878–1879) ——————→

Nordenskjöld's winter camp   ⊗

[dark] Permanent sea ice

[medium] Seas and lakes frozen in winter

[light] Open sea

Nordenskjöld's navigation of the Northeast Passage (above) took him around the top of the world. contribution to the charting of the Arctic, however, was to prove it was possible to sail to the Pacific through the Northeast Passage, which had already been charted by a Russian expedition. He set out in July 1878 on the *Vega* and by September had almost reached the Bering Strait

THE SKILLS OF THE ESKIMOS

There was no new technology to help 19th-century explorers overcome the hardships of the Arctic. In fact the key to success was to adopt the survival techniques of the Eskimos who lived in the Arctic.

These hardy people had watched such luckless adventurers as Sir John Franklin perish where they themselves survived. Eskimos ate whales, seals, and fish, all of which they were expert in catching. For shelter they built tents of animal skins or huts (igloos) of snow bricks and wore the fur of caribou to keep warm. They were skilled in the use of dogs to draw sleds over the ice. Eskimos also knew their own territory well; they would sometimes draw useful maps for visiting explorers.

Wolfgang Kaehler/Corbis

between Alaska and eastern Siberia. This channel offered a gateway to the Pacific—but the *Vega* became frozen in, and the expedition spent the winter in Siberia. In July 1879 the ice finally yielded; the crew got up steam, and the ship cruised triumphantly into the Pacific. Nordenskjöld had proved it was possible to navigate through the Northeast Passage.

THE FATE OF THE *JEANNETTE*

Just as Nordenskjöld was entering the Pacific, yet another American expedition was setting out from San Francisco. The *Jeannette*, with a crew of 33, was captained by a naval officer, George De Long. De Long had planned to meet Nordenskjöld, as their paths ought to have crossed. But he ran into trouble: the *Jeannette* became trapped in the ice in September 1879. The ship was carried by the drift for a year and a half before it broke up and sank in October 1881. De Long and his crew made a desperate bid for land, but few survived. Although the trip ended in tragedy, De Long did not die in vain: his diaries were recovered, and the account of his amazing journey caught in the ice gave later explorers an understanding of the Arctic seas.

THE RACE IS ON!

Although in the 1880s geographical and scientific studies of the Arctic continued, explorers grew ever more eager to be first at the Pole. In 1882 Adolphus Greely, an American Army officer, reached as far as 83° 24' North, beating the former record held by Nares.

Greely's record was beaten in 1895 by the Norwegian Fridtjof Nansen, a zoologist and keen student of Eskimo life. Nansen was one of the great Arctic explorers: he had crossed Greenland on skis and was fascinated by the enormous polar wastes. When he heard that De Long's ship, the *Jeannette*, had been

Hulton Getty

carried thousands of miles in the sea ice to the coast of Greenland, Nansen hit on a daring plan. He decided to build a ship strong enough to withstand the mighty crush of ice, sail into the frozen sea, and let its flow carry him to within striking distance of the North Pole. This ship was to be the *Fram*.

CONSIDERED CRAZY

Although his plan was widely considered to be crazy, Nansen acquired financial backing and commissioned his ship. With its three masts of sail and stubby, bathtub shape, the 402-ton *Fram* was

In this portrait (above) Nils Nordenskjöld looks every inch a hero of the Arctic. But he was also a trained scientist and was eager to discover the true nature of the far north.

Left: When the Jeannette sank off Siberia in 1881, the crew made a six-week trek over the ice before setting sail for the mainland in three boats. Only one party survived.

Below: Mile by mile, the Arctic expeditions of the late 19th century pushed closer to the North Pole.

Hulton Getty

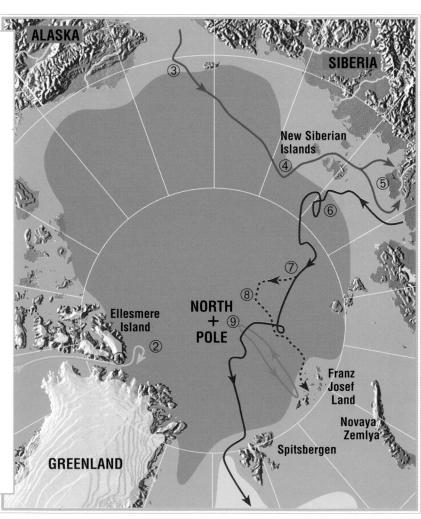

NORTH POLAR EXPEDITIONS 1875-1900

Nares (1875–1876)

De Long (1879–1881)

Nansen (1893–1896)

Amedeo (1900)

Permanent sea ice

Seas and lakes frozen in winter

Open sea

① Nares's winter quarters, 1875
② Nares's farthest point, May 1876
③ The *Jeannette* caught in the ice, September 1879
④ The *Jeannette* abandoned in ice, 1881
⑤ *Jeannette's* survivors reach Siberia, 1881
⑥ The *Fram* locked in ice and drifting north, September 1893
⑦ Nansen sets out overland, March 1895
⑧ Nansen turns back—makes for Franz Josef Land
⑨ Farthest point of Amedeo's expedition, April 1900

ALASKA
SIBERIA
New Siberian Islands
NORTH + POLE
Ellesmere Island
Franz Josef Land
Novaya Zemlya
Spitsbergen
GREENLAND

Wolfgang Faehler/Corbis

Above: The Arctic pack ice had long been feared as a menace to shipping. So when Fridtjof Nansen actually planned for his ship to get stuck in the ice and drift toward the North Pole, people thought he had lost his mind. In fact, his "crazy" plan very nearly succeeded.

certainly no beauty, but her specially shaped and reinforced hull was designed to resist the pressure of the ice and to rise out of the ice when frozen in. The rounded hull, constructed from oak, pitch pine, and greenheart timbers, was up to 28 inches (70 cm) thick in places. A three-cylinder engine, when used together with full sail, gave the *Fram* a top speed of seven knots.

Nansen left Oslo in the *Fram* in June 1893. By September he and his ship were firmly locked in the ice. Nansen and his crew lived aboard ship for a year, drifting slowly northward.

The drift was, however, too slow for Nansen. He left the ship in March 1895 accompanied by the ship's stoker, Frederik Johansen, and headed for the

North Pole with three dog sleds. Nansen's diaries reveal his fondness for the stocky ship: "It is like bidding farewell to a dear friend and to a home, which has long afforded me a sheltering

---

With her stubby, bathtub shape, the 402-ton Fram was certainly no beauty.

---

roof; at one blow all this and my dear comrades are to be left behind forever."

Nansen entrusted the *Fram* to the capable hands of Otto Sverdrup. Held in the grip of the ice, the ship drifted to Spitsbergen before finally breaking free. Although the *Fram* had not drifted in the direction Nansen expected, it was a remarkable exploit in which he succeeded in charting the depth of the sea ice in the Arctic.

Nansen and Johansen had to turn back just 240 miles (385 km) from the Pole. As they could not find the ship, they set off overland. They reached Franz Josef Land in July 1895, where they survived the winter hunting polar bears and walruses. Nearly a year later they met the British explorer Frederick Jackson, who was surveying the area. Jackson had anticipated this reunion, bringing letters from Nansen's wife and the Norwegian government. He had been looking out for a tall, slim, and fair-haired man, and it was some moments before he recognized the wild-looking character in filthy rags, with oil-

blackened hair and a paunch from his fatty diet of Arctic mammals.

Five years later in 1900 an Italian expedition led by Luigi Amedeo, Duke of Abruzzi, sledded to a record latitude of 86° 34' North. Robert Peary, an American naval officer, set another record in 1906 before he was forced to turn back, beaten by great ridges of ice. But Peary was destined to return.

Left: The Fram returned home to a jubilant welcome after her epic voyage. Her exploration days, however, were not over: Amundsen used her in 1910 for his conquest of the South Pole.

Hulton Getty

HOW PACK ICE IS FORMED

Pack ice (below) is formed when, in freezing temperatures, the top few inches of the sea begin to freeze into thin plates of ice. Freezing continues on the undersides of these plates until, eventually, rafts of ice several feet thick are formed.

Wind and currents keep the rafts moving and prevent them from forming a solid sheet; they also cause the rafts to collide and ride up onto each other. This results in a ridged, uneven surface that makes it very difficult to make progress on foot. To make matters worse for explorers with sleds, the pack ice opens up in places to expose stretches of water, known as leads.

Shipping can, today, penetrate the pack ice, but a sudden freeze can bring great danger. The pack ice locks up in the bitter polar winters, and such is the pressure caused by the expanding ice that a ship can be crushed like a nut in the sea's viselike grip.

The limits of the pack ice advance and retreat with the passing seasons. On average, the Arctic Ocean contains more than four million square miles (almost 11 million sq km) of pack ice. The seas around Antarctica contain about twice this amount—a coverage of about 8 percent of the southern hemisphere's total surface.

The Hutchison Library

CONQUERING THE NORTH

Fridtjof Nansen's journey on the *Fram* in 1893 created much enthusiasm in his native Norway for Arctic exploration. Nansen himself was exhausted, but his ship was still intact, and its captain Otto Sverdrup was eager to set out again.

Sverdrup was a highly skilled explorer, and his personal successes are often overshadowed by those of his more famous countryman. He had skied across Greenland with Nansen in 1888 and had captained the *Fram* after Nansen left her to try for the North Pole. Two years later he took command of the *Fram* once again for an expedition, supported by the Norwegian government, to northern Greenland. From 1898 to 1902 he researched the wildlife of the Arctic and mapped extensive areas. A newly discovered group of islands was named after him, and the west of Ellesmere Island was named King Oscar Land after the Norwegian king.

AMUNDSEN AND THE *GJOA*

Meanwhile a young Norwegian, Roald Amundsen, had been training to be an explorer. He had studied magnetism in the earth in Germany, learned seamanship in a sailing vessel, and taken part in seal-hunting trips. He had also joined the Belgian explorer Baron de Gerlache de Gomery on an expedition to the Antarctic in 1897. There, he took command of the icebound ship *Belgica* and saved the party from scurvy and starvation by his knowledge of survival techniques.

Now Amundsen equipped a small Norwegian fishing boat, the *Gjoa*, and set out in June 1903 to sail from the Atlantic

With their extra warm fur coats polar bears (right) are at home in the freezing climate of the Arctic Circle (below).

to the Pacific through the Northwest Passage. On the way he was icebound several times and took the opportunity to explore far-northern Canada. He and Sverdrup contributed to a major mapping of previously unknown territories. Finally, Amundsen brought the *Gjoa* through to the Pacific and arrived in San

Francisco in October 1906, where he donated the ship to the city. He bought Nansen's *Fram* in 1908, planning to return to the Arctic and once more allow the boat to drift toward the Pole.

But Amundsen abandoned his plans when he learned that another explorer—from the United States—had already

Dan Guravich/Corbis

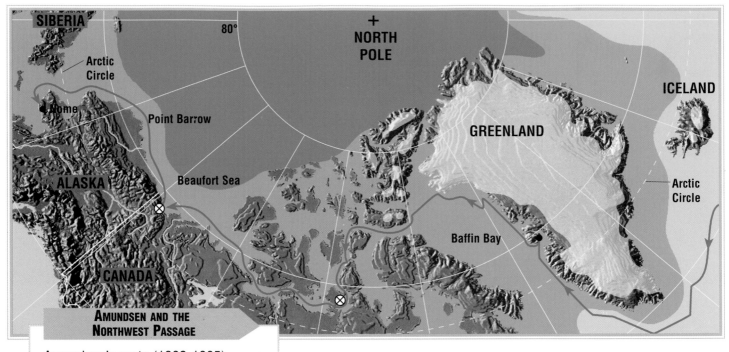

AMUNDSEN AND THE
NORTHWEST PASSAGE

Amundsen's route (1903-1905) ———→

Amundsen's winter camps ⊗

Permanent sea ice

Seas and lakes frozen in winter

Open sea

reached the Pole. In fact, two Americans had made the claim, but only one received full honors for it in one of the most intriguing stories of polar exploration.

FIRST ACROSS THE LINE?

Born in Pennsylvania, Robert Peary studied engineering before joining the navy in 1881. A fiercely competitive man, he had a burning ambition to do something memorable in his life. Having read accounts of Nils Nordenskjöld's polar exploration, he determined to claim what he considered "the last great geographical prize"—conquest of the North Pole.

Roald Amundsen (right) followed in the footsteps of his hero, Fridtjof Nansen, to become the world's most renowned polar explorer.

Peary's Arctic adventures began in 1886 when, as a 30-year-old, he tried to cross Greenland. He failed but, undeterred, returned in 1891 to lead a party for the Philadelphia Academy of Natural Sciences. On the way he broke his leg and was treated by Dr. Frederick Albert Cook, the medical officer on his ship the *Kite*. That winter Peary learned survival techniques from the Eskimos.

When Peary heard that Sverdrup was setting out for the Arctic in 1888, he was convinced that the Norwegians were aiming for the Pole. (He was, in fact, wrong: Sverdrup was interested only in research.) So Peary redoubled his efforts to get there first, and in a series of expeditions he got progressively closer and closer to the Pole.

> **Robert Peary was convinced that the Norwegians were planning to race him to the North Pole.**

In 1898 a wealthy New York syndicate formed the Peary Arctic Club to finance his explorations. In 1904 the club raised the money to buy him a new ship, the *Roosevelt*, which was specially designed to force a way through the ice. When the ship sailed in 1905, Peary was already 50 years old and had lost eight toes through frostbite. But he had developed a unique expertise in travel over the Arctic wastes and was sure of his abilities.

TRAVELING BY SLED

Once the ship was left behind, the journey was extremely hazardous, for the men would have to cross more than 400

Robert Peary owed his success—if indeed he reached the Pole—to his reliance on Eskimo techniques.

Hulton Getty/Corbis

miles (640 km) of sea ice. The Arctic is no smooth ice rink but an unstable mass in which pressure ridges of ice rise as high as houses, snow piles up into drifts, and the movement of the frozen sea opens up gaps of clear icy water that sleds cannot cross. Terrible blizzards can blow for days on end. And all the time readings

EMERGENCY RATIONS

In the early days of polar exploration, success or failure often depended on the choice of food. An explorer could burn up half a pound of body fat every day in the Arctic, and high-energy foodstuffs—chocolate, sugar, biscuits, and pemmican (dried meat and fat)—were essential to restore body reserves.

On many an expedition, however, delays occurred which exhausted food supplies. Explorers would then have to hunt seals, walruses (below), and bears, using guns, harpoons, or knives. A lucky potshot at such prey saved many a hungry explorer from starvation. In 1884 Adolphus Greely was one of six half-starved survivors from a U.S. Army expedition to the Arctic. On this expedition 19 men died of starvation after resorting to eating boiled sealskin clothing for food.

Wolfgang Kaehler/Corbis

Dan Guravich/Corbis

have to be taken and positions checked, for it is all too easy to drift off course on the moving rafts of ice.

Peary knew all about these hazards and relied heavily on Eskimo expertise. When he set out for the Pole in July 1906 he took a hand-picked team. This included his African-American valet Matthew Hensen. A farmer's son from Maryland, Hensen had gone to sea at the age of 12 and traveled the world. Having worked for Peary from 1887, he had become expert in sled navigation.

A team of Eskimos was recruited—men, women, and children. It was they who drove the dog teams (there were more than a hundred dogs on this trip), built igloos—which were much warmer than tents—and made coats from seal and walrus skins for the party to wear. Advance parties on the route to the Pole set up camps, built igloos, and left stores, so that the final assault team would waste no time if the weather was fair. It was a brilliant system evolved from years of meticulous planning.

However, the weather could still ruin the best-laid plans. Peary was slowed down by temperatures as low as –60° F (–51° C). All he managed to do was break the world record for getting nearest the Pole, and he nearly died in the attempt. When he returned to the *Roosevelt,* captained by Bob Bartlett, the ship had been badly damaged in the pack ice and had to return to New York for repairs.

The Peary Arctic Club paid the bill, and in July 1908 Peary was once again on his way with Hensen, Bartlett, and

Time and again dogs proved to be the best for hauling sleds across the ice. But they could be unruly, and it took an experienced driver to win their respect and work them successfully.

three others. Frederick Cook was not among them: he would shortly head for the Pole himself. In Greenland Peary took on 50 Eskimos with 250 dogs, and in February 1909 the party set out, setting up camps on the ice. By April 1 he was only 150 miles (240 km) from victory.

THE FINAL ASSAULT

The question arose of who should be in the final assault. So far, Peary had kept Bob Bartlett with him (he had in 1905 promised the man a place in the final party), but he unexpectedly ordered Bartlett back to the ship. Peary, now accompanied only by Hensen and four Eskimos, was utterly determined to be the first explorer to reach the Pole.

By his own account Peary reached the Pole on April 6, 1909, and claimed the entire region for the president of the United States. He planted flags for the U.S., the Navy League, the Red Cross, the World's Ensign of Liberty and Peace, and for his

Native Arctic hunters (below) trained Robert Peary to live off the land. These Eskimos are catching a seal; once harpooned, the wounded animal could be hauled in with the line.

DID PEARY REACH THE POLE?

To this day, no one can prove for certain that Robert Peary really reached the North Pole. Of his Arctic survival and planning skills, his bravery, physical power, and cast-iron determination, there was no doubt. But many unanswered questions about the final assault led some people to believe that Peary may have lied to the world about his achievement.

First, it was known that Peary was desperate to succeed. In 1909, the year of his final attempt, he was aged 53 and lame. One more failure might be the final blow for his financers, who had spent huge sums on his many trips. His jealous and competitive character, which could surface in his unsportsmanlike dismissal of other men's achievements, was notorious among exploration circles.

When he ordered Bartlett to turn back, Peary was effectively removing the last man who could prove him right or wrong. Only Matt Henson and four Eskimos accompanied him on the last stretch. Although capable of taking readings from the navigation instruments, these men were unable to make the complex calculations—Peary alone could do so. And even if they

Peary claimed the Pole on April 6, 1909. The Eskimos built an igloo at the site, which he crowned with an American flag.

Hulton Getty

could have proved that he did not reach the Pole, their word would have been of little use—because in 1909 the testimony of non-whites would have carried very little weight.

Peary's diary entries raise many uncomfortable questions. In them he claimed to have covered the final 150 miles (240 km) in five days, at an average rate of nearly 30 miles (48 km) a day. This was unbelievably fast. When he finally stopped on April 6, at a point he cautiously announced to be the last and most northerly camp on the Earth, he refused—for the very first time—to allow Henson to take any readings. That day he did not specifically claim to have reached the Pole. His diary pages for April 7 and 8 are also blank, and the page on which he celebrated "the Pole at last!!!" is a loose-leaf, undated sheet of a different kind of paper.

Many other questions, concerning Peary's route, his navigation, and his overall manner, remain unanswered. Although he successfully fought Frederick Cook's competing claim, a shadow of doubt still hangs over his version of the events that shook the world in April 1909.

Frederick Cook (above) claimed to have reached the Pole before Peary.

WHERE IS THE NORTH POLE?

The geographic North Pole lies at the northernmost point of the Earth. On a map of the Arctic it is the point at which all the lines of longitude meet. It is always found at 90° North, 0° West, and is exactly opposite the South Pole in Antarctica. However, because the North Pole is not found on dry land, but lies amid the drifting pack ice on the Arctic Ocean (below), its location cannot be permanently marked. In the words of Wally Herbert, a British explorer who reached the North Pole in 1969, "Trying to set foot upon [the North Pole] was like trying to step on the shadow of a bird that was circling overhead."

The magnetic North Pole is an even more complex matter, for unlike the geographic Pole, it is not represented by a fixed point on a map. Its movement arises from the Earth's daily rotation around the polar axis. As the Earth rotates, it is made magnetic. The movement also disturbs molten rock at the planet's core. The magnetized molten rock, over long periods of time, causes the magnetic axis to shift. Currently, the magnetic North Pole is located 800 miles (1,250 km) from the geographic North Pole, in the Northwest Territories of Canada.

college fraternity. He left a capsule with a strip of the American flag, a record of his journey, and accreditation to the Peary Arctic Club. He noted how strange it was that when he and two Eskimos sledded in a straight line from one side of the Pole to the other, they first traveled north and then south, and that the wind, wherever it blew, was always a south wind.

Exhausted, Peary returned with his party to the *Roosevelt*—only to receive shattering news. Frederick Cook had visited five days earlier, claiming that he had reached the North Pole a year earlier on April 21, 1908. Cook had then found a ship to take him to Denmark and, before Peary could announce his triumph to the world, had already claimed the victory laurels for himself.

Denouncing Cook as a charlatan, Peary fought bitterly for his own claim, but the world of exploration became divided: who was telling the truth? Cook's scientific notebooks were lost, and there was no evidence to establish whether his claims were justified. In the end it was Peary who received the medals and awards for being the first white man at the North Pole, though great doubts remained about the truthfulness of his diary entries and observations.

SCIENTIFIC RESEARCH AND MAPPING

This squabble marked the end of the race for the North Pole, and explorers turned their attention to more useful scientific research and mapping. Above all, there was a much greater interest in the native peoples of the Arctic.

One such research expedition was made by the Danish explorer Ludvic Mylius-Erichsen, who, in 1906, took a team of scientists to the northeast coast of Greenland. His distinguished passengers included Einar Mikkelsen, Knud Rasmussen, and Alfred Wegener. These scientists contributed greatly to the un-

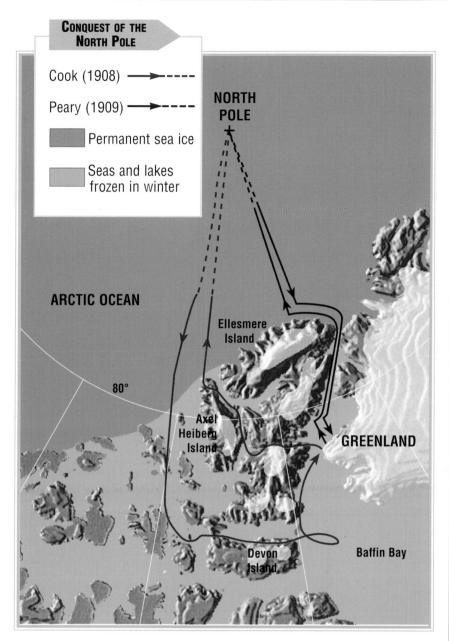

CONQUEST OF THE NORTH POLE

Cook (1908) ━━▶ ┄┄┄

Peary (1909) ━━▶ ┄┄┄

Permanent sea ice

Seas and lakes frozen in winter

NORTH POLE

ARCTIC OCEAN

Ellesmere Island

80°

Axel Heiberg Island

GREENLAND

Devon Island

Baffin Bay

The routes of Cook and Peary in their polar bids (above).

Most British Arctic explorers took heavy sleeping bags. Not so Peary (right), who slept and traveled in thick furs.

Popperfoto

Spitsbergen (above), a cluster of islands far to the north of Scandinavia, lies close to the outer limits of the permanent Arctic sea ice. Several polar expeditions set off from, and returned to, its icy shores.

derstanding of the Arctic and its people. The first European to discover the long peninsula at the north of Greenland, Mylius-Erichsen made several other valuable observations (many of which actually proved Peary's maps to be wrong). Sadly, Mylius-Erichsen and two companions died of cold and starvation.

Their bodies and his notes were found by expeditions that went in search of them, the most remarkable of which was led by Einar Mikkelsen. Mikkelsen very nearly perished himself and was presumed to have died before he was found, half-crazy and terribly emaciated, by

Norwegian sealers. He had spent two winters in the Arctic with little food and no fuel; his party had eaten all their dogs before the first winter was out.

STEFANSSON'S SUCCESS

From the late 19th century to the outbreak of the First World War in 1914 understanding of the Arctic's geography and climate advanced steadily. As war raged in Europe, one final, highly successful expedition set out from Canada led by Vilhjalmur Stefansson.

Stefansson was born in Manitoba, Canada, but his parents originally came

THE NORTHERN LIGHTS

One of the most spectacular sights of the polar regions is a stunning light show known as an aurora. In the Northern Hemisphere this is known as the aurora borealis, or northern lights; in the southern hemisphere it is called the aurora australis, or southern lights.

On a clear night, the sky is filled with vivid bands and patches of color; these may appear motionless for hours, or ripple and flash like the lighting display at a rock concert. The British explorer George Lyon, who commanded the *Hecla* on her Arctic voyage of 1821–1822, described pulsing showers of light rays "like those thrown from a rocket," and glowing displays "like wondrous showers of fire."

Auroras occur when energy from the sun enters our atmosphere and is drawn, by the Earth's magnetism, to the polar regions. The particles of solar energy strike oxygen and nitrogen atoms. Atomic particles known as ions then become highly charged, and produce the glowing colors of the aurora. Very occasionally, when solar winds are particularly strong, auroras can be seen as far south as the United States.

from Iceland. After leaving college he spent several years living with native tribes—including the Inuit of Coronation Gulf, who had never before met white men. He was chosen to lead a scientific team on the Canadian Arctic Expedition of 1913–1918 exploring uncharted islands within the Arctic Circle.

But disaster befell the expedition's principal ship, the *Karluk*. As she rounded Point Barrow in the pack ice, she was swept away and wrecked. The survivors included the captain, Bob Bartlett, as well as Stefansson and Hubert Wilkins, who had been hunting on the ice.

Undaunted, the Canadian expedition spent five winters in the Arctic. They set up a research station on a sheet of moving ice 15 miles (24 km) long that drifted for 400 miles (640 km) as they recorded data. When the expedition returned in 1918, it had charted a huge area of the Canadian Arctic archipelago.

Wayne R. Bilenduke/Tony Stone Images

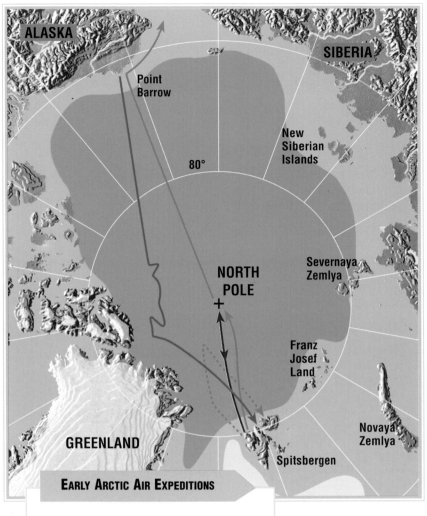

EARLY ARCTIC AIR EXPEDITIONS

Amundsen and Ellsworth (1925) ----►

Byrd (1926) ──────►

Amundsen (airship) (1926) ───►

Wilkins (1928) ──────►

Permanent sea ice

Seas and lakes frozen in winter

The American aviator Richard Byrd was the first to reach the North Pole by air in 1926. The map above shows his route, together with those of other air explorers.

Library of Congress/Corbis

in the First World War, and he offered to team up with Amundsen to help fund, equip, and pilot an attempt on the North Pole.

Ellsworth provided two German Dornier-Whale seaplanes with Rolls-Royce engines. They took off from Spitsbergen and got within 120 miles (192 km) of the North Pole before one of the planes developed a problem and had to land. The other was damaged when it landed on the uneven ice. Although they failed to fly over the Pole, they did manage to survey from the air some 12,000 square miles (31,000 sq km) and returned safely in one of the planes.

A year later an American naval officer, Richard Byrd, attempted the same trip.

RICHARD E. BYRD
Byrd was from a wealthy family in Winchester, Virginia, and had trained as a naval flier in the First World War. He had also taken part in one of the earliest

Arctic airborne surveys in 1924–1925 as part of an exploration of Greenland. He and the pilot Floyd Bennett had flown many times over the fringes of the Arctic.

In April 1926 Byrd sailed to Spitsbergen on the *Chantier*, taking with him a Fokker F-VII monoplane and his pilot Floyd Bennett. For the last part of

Amundsen and Ellsworth practice leading dog sleds in Alaska in 1925 (above), before attempting to fly to the Pole.

Museum of Flight/Corbis

Above: For his attempt on the North Pole Richard Byrd used a German Fokker F-VII three-engined monoplane.

the journey the plane had to be lifted onto boats and hauled along, as the *Chantier* was stuck fast in the ice.

Byrd made three attempts to take off and crashed each time, wrecking all the spare landing gear, and had to fashion a makeshift set of skis from oars. Then, in fine weather on May 9, 1926, he and his

pilot finally took off. After taking some bearings and overcoming an oil-leak scare, they headed for the Pole. They found it, circled for a while, and then flew safely back to Spitsbergen.

The trip of 1,440 miles (2,300 km) had taken 16 hours: Byrd had maintained an average speed of 90 mph (144 km/h). The most that Robert Peary had managed with his dog teams and sleds was 30 miles (48 km) a day.

AMUNDSEN AND THE *NORGE*

Roald Amundsen was there when Byrd made his triumphant return, and he congratulated the American who had beaten him to a first in polar exploration. But Amundsen was not a mere spectator. He was on Spitsbergen awaiting the arrival of a great airship or dirigible—the *Norge*—in which he had hoped to be the first to fly over the Pole.

On May 12, 1926, three days after Byrd's flight to the North Pole, Amundsen took off in the *Norge* with Lincoln Ellsworth and the airship's designer, the Italian Umberto Nobile.

WINGS OVER THE ICE

The airplanes that first carried explorers to the Poles were much smaller and cruder than today's jet planes. They were lightweight and powered by internal combustion engines. The cabins were cold, and the aviators had to wear fur jackets, helmets, and boots to keep themselves from freezing. But some airplanes proved their worth time and again, such as the German Fokker F-VII used by Richard Byrd to reach the North Pole in 1926.

Taking off from the Arctic pack ice—even in a sturdy prize-winner such as the F-VII—was not easy. Fires had to be lighted to thin the oil for lubrication, and a runway had to be hammered out of rough ice. The plane took off on skis rather than wheels, and although these were useful for landing on soft snow, they were easily smashed by the uneven surface.

The three had none of the hapless Andrée's difficulties at first and were over the North Pole in good time; they threw down their national flags as they drifted over the ice.

But then the going got tougher: their radio ceased to work, and the nose and ropes of the *Norge* became covered in ice. Though navigation was difficult, they managed to get to Alaska, flying 3,400 miles (5,440 km) in two and a half days.

The Alaskan Eskimos, peering up at the *Norge*, likened the mighty airship to a "flying whale."

However, once they were back at base, Amundsen and Nobile fought, and a bitter argument over the credit for the trip raged in the newspapers. Amundsen declared that Nobile was pompous and a hopeless navigator, and that his airship was poorly designed. This was a little unfair, since Nobile knew a great deal

Although the Norge (below) made it to the Pole, Amundsen and Nobile later parted in anger, the Norwegian complaining that Nobile was a poor designer and navigator.

OBSERVATION FROM THE AIR

Aerial photography dates from 1858, when a French experimenter took pictures of Paris from his hot-air balloon. From the late 1920s the Arctic was mapped out by systematic aerial photography. Pilots on polar flights would fly up and down in overlapping lines—rather as a tractor plows a field—taking hundreds of photographs. These pictures were then carefully patched together to create complete images of the remote terrain.

more than Amundsen about airship design. Angered by this slur, and to show he was the master of polar flight, Nobile persuaded the Italian dictator Mussolini to back an Italian polar expedition. Nobile also got public donations and assistance from Britain's Royal

Below: Byrd, returning to Spitsbergen after flying over the Pole, is congratulated by Amundsen.

Geographical Society. He designed a new, and so he believed, much better airship—the *Italia*—especially for exploration of the Arctic.

WILKINS FLIES OVER THE ARCTIC

Just before the *Italia* took off in May 1928, the Australian George Wilkins achieved his ambition, after many failed attempts, to fly across the Arctic in an airplane from west to east.

Wilkins was already an experienced polar explorer. He had been second in command to Vilhjalmur Stefansson in the Canadian Arctic Expedition of 1913–1918 and had taken part in British Antarctic expeditions. In an earlier attempt to overfly the Arctic he had crashed and had had to survive for several days before he was rescued. But

he was convinced that air travel would one day conquer this region and that commercial airlines would fly over it.

Wilkins's pioneer crossing began on April 15, 1928, when he flew from Point Barrow, Alaska, in the west to—or almost to—Spitsbergen in the east. Wilkins and his copilot Carl Eielson flew to within sight of Spitsbergen after a flight lasting

---

> ### With Wilkins helping to push the plane with one foot, they finally took off.

---

20 hours and 20 minutes, when they managed to land the plane on an outlying island. It took them a week to get going again, but they managed to take off with Wilkins helping to push the plane into the air with one foot, and completed their historic trip half an hour later.

THE FLIGHT OF THE *ITALIA*

The flight of Nobile's airship *Italia* began a few weeks later on May 23, 1928. The intention was to land at the North Pole, make some soundings, and return to

Mary Evans Picture Library

Above: Umberto Nobile and his Italia *airship, 1928.*

Corbis/UPI/Bettmann

LOUISE BOYD

One of those who joined the search for Amundsen in 1928 after his seaplane crashed in the Arctic was a remarkable American explorer, Louise Boyd. Boyd came from a wealthy Californian family. Her parents died when she was 33, and she inherited a fortune. She spent much of it on adventures in the Arctic, often with a party of friends, and with sponsorship from the American Geographical Society. She played an important part in advising her government on Arctic strategy in the Second World War. On her final Arctic expedition in 1955 Boyd became the first woman to fly over the North Pole—at the ripe old age of 68.

Spitsbergen. By the time they reached the Pole, however, the airship was weighed down with ice, and the radio had broken down. Nobile threw out the Italian flag and a wooden cross given to him by the Pope, who had blessed the airship. He decided to head back to base without risking a landing.

Then disaster struck. Covered in ice and enshrouded by freezing fog, the *Italia* was tilting downward at the stern, and Nobile was powerless to stabilize it. Eventually, it was forced down onto the ice 180 miles (290 km) from Spitsbergen. The impact smashed the pilot car, killing one man and badly injuring Nobile. Having jettisoned some of its human cargo in the crash, the *Italia* suddenly rose, and seven men in another car were carried off into the bleak Arctic fog. They were never to be seen again. Nobile, with a fractured arm and leg, was left with

OTTO SCHMIDT

In 1932 the Russian scientist Otto Schmidt (below, center) was put in charge of a Russian unit looking for a way through the Northeast Passage. He took the icebreaker *Sibiryakov* from Murmansk to Vladivostok in just over two months—the first time a ship had got through in one season. He then tried to accomplish the round trip in a year with a party of 100 people, including women and children, but his ship was wrecked by pack ice. Luckily, nearly everyone survived to be airlifted out.

Schmidt's most spectacular exploit was his attempt to set up the first manned scientific station at the North Pole. Men and supplies were flown out and deposited close to the Pole from May 1937, and a group of researchers remained at the base while Schmidt returned to Franz Josef Land.

However, the drift of the pack ice soon carried the research station toward the east coast of Greenland. By February 1938 the station had drifted 1,500 miles (2,400 km) from the Pole. Alerted by a radio message, a rescue party picked up the researchers just before their ice raft broke up.

Hulton Getty

Umberto Nobile (right) was desperate to prove his own expertise and the usefulness of his airships— but the disastrous 1928 flight of the Italia *failed him on both counts.*

three of the crew. They managed to fix the radio and send out a distress signal.

TO THE RESCUE

There followed a huge international rescue operation. Amundsen was asked by the Norwegian government to join in, and he set off in a French seaplane to search for the man he had quarreled with so bitterly not long before. Somewhere in the Arctic Amundsen crashed, and only remnants of his plane were found. It was a tragic end for an explorer who had traveled to the ends of the Earth.

> **Amundsen flew off to search for Nobile—but somewhere in the Arctic he crashed.**

Eventually a Swedish pilot found the stranded party, but his plane could carry only one passenger. The injured Nobile was taken away first. The pilot damaged his plane when returning for a second trip, and the others were eventually picked up by a Russian icebreaker.

Because Nobile allowed himself to be the first taken to safety, Mussolini had him arrested for deserting his men. Forced to leave Italy, Nobile spent many years in Russia and later the United States, until he was cleared of charges after the Second World War.

DANGER IN THE AIR

Arctic exploration in the air had proved to be extremely dangerous. But some of the pioneers of airborne expeditions in the North had a key role in the opening up of Antarctica.

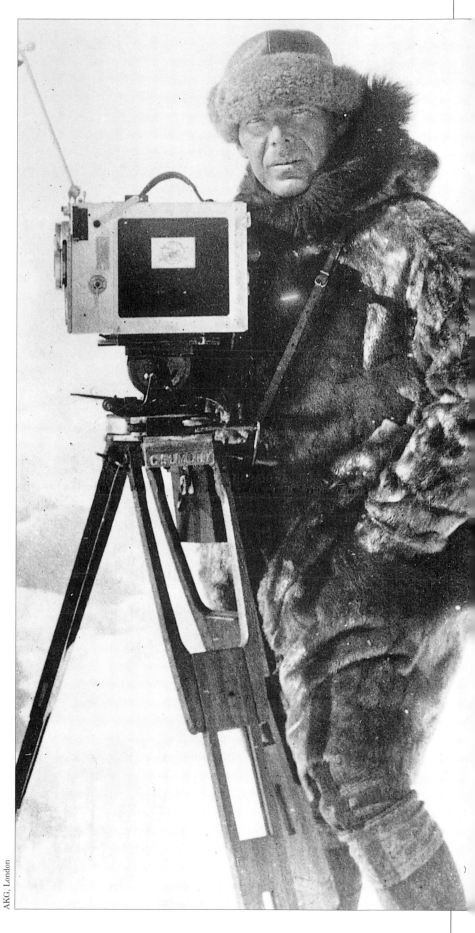

AKG, London

ANTARCTICA:
THE GREAT
UNKNOWN

The Arctic Ocean has claimed the lives of many explorers, but for all its wild and inhospitable character it cannot compete with the desolation and fury of the southern polar region. The Antarctic, a vast area of about five million square miles (over 13 million sq. km), is the most hostile region of our planet.

Antarctica was the last great continent to be explored by humans. It has no native peoples, and there are no native land mammals. Only such hardy birds as penguins, and an abundance of seals and whales in the coastal waters, can brave the murderous conditions.

Whereas the Arctic fringes are the northernmost regions of North America, Europe, and Asia, Antarctica lies hundreds of miles south of any other continental mainland. The southern seas are whipped into waves as high as houses. Any vessel that approaches Antarctica must sail through rafts of pack ice. In a storm these iron-hard rock-like lumps of ice are tossed about—a deadly hazard for shipping.

A PROMISED LAND
In the mid 18th century some fanciful ideas existed about Antarctica. Many people believed that to the south of the southern oceans there was a land rich in vegetation and wildlife. They dreamed of another North America waiting to be discovered by those brave enough to explore beyond the wild seas.

Penguins (right) are among the few living creatures adapted to survive the inhospitable Antarctic climate.

Isabella Tree/The Hutchison Library

However by the 19th century it was evident that such a land could not exist. Great sea captains—including James Cook in the late 18th century—had sailed south among the icebergs that infest the seas around Antarctica; they had sighted what they believed was land, but it did not look inviting at all. Cook had spotted frozen rocks in the icebergs, which suggested there was land there—but of a distinctly bleak kind.

> *Captain Cook had noted large numbers of seals and whales in the southern seas.*

Sir James Ross had traveled to Antarctica in the 1840s in search of the magnetic South Pole (he had found the

Sir James Ross discovered and named the volcano Mount Erebus (below) in the 1840s.

magnetic North Pole 10 years before). He identified some islands and named the great volcano he found Mount Erebus after his ship and another peak, Mount Terror, after her sister ship. He had located what became known as the Ross Ice Shelf, a vast shelf of frozen water jutting out over the sea from mainland Antarctica, and McMurdo Sound, named after an officer on the *Terror*.

WHALING IN THE SOUTH SEAS

Captain Cook had noted numbers of seals and whales in the southern seas, and this attracted the attention of whalers. There was by then a huge industry in skins and oil, and commercial ships sailed toward Antarctica in droves.

At first it was just the seal population that was plundered mercilessly. Then, within a few decades, the Norwegians revolutionized the whaling business with steamships and harpoon guns, and the whalers also turned to the Antarctic to claim the natural bounty. Their crews

Hulton Getty

Nigel Sitwell/The Hutchison Library

had no wish to venture far inland, however. Their bounty was on ice floes and in the waters of the region.

So at the beginning of the 20th century mainland Antarctica was the world's last great unexplored region. But it was destined to yield its secrets in the space of a few years: much had been learned in the Arctic in the way of exploration techniques, and scientists followed hot on the heels of the southbound whalers.

VOYAGE OF THE *ANTARCTIC*

It fell to the Norwegians, the champions of modern whaling, to make the first extensive land exploration of Antarctica. Carl Larsen, a whaler captain, made a first trip in 1893; he then returned to Norway to raise funds for an expedition.

In a refitted ship, the *Antarctic*, he sailed for Melbourne, Australia. There, the ship's manager, a young Norwegian

by the name of Henryk Bull, had hoped to pick up a group of scientist-explorers from Europe. But they arrived too late, and the *Antarctic* took instead Carsten Borchgrevink. A Norwegian who had settled in Australia, he was a teacher and scientist with a thirst for adventure.

Seals (above) were hunted when rations ran low; one explorer even enjoyed seal's blood pancakes!

THE ANTARCTIC WINTER

Lying at the ends of the Earth, the poles receive less sunlight than any other region. The Arctic may be icy—but Antarctica is inhumanly cold, with the worst winter in the world.

In the Antarctic winter the sun disappears for four months—from May to August—and winds can blow at hurricane force for days on end. The Antarctic is isolated from the rest of the world's climate by low-pressure systems in the southern seas, and the temperature has been known to plummet as low as −128.6°F (−89.2°C)—almost unimaginably cold.

The expedition left Australia in 1894, and the *Antarctic* managed to penetrate the pack ice to the shores of what had, from a distance, been named Victoria Land. In January 1895, a party took a boat to go ashore, and Borchgrevink made a few forays into the mainland.

THE *SOUTHERN CROSS*

After this expedition Borchgrevink visited Britain, where he persuaded a wealthy magazine publisher to back a new venture. It was to be a great story— the first man to spend a winter on mainland Antarctica. Britain's Royal Geographical Society opposed the idea, predicting that it would end in disaster.

Borchgrevink wanted to be the first man to spend a winter on Antarctica.

Borchgrevink's new ship, the *Southern Cross*, sailed from London in August 1898 with a team of scientists on board. He also took sled dogs, and two Laplanders from Finland to drive them. By January 1899 the ship was nosing through the pack ice and on February 17 found a landing point. Borchgrevink set up camp near the site of his previous landing on Antarctica four years earlier.

On March 1, 1899, the British flag was raised over what was named Camp Ridley, a hut with a roof of canvas and seal skins held down with sacks of coal. Borchgrevink set up observatories to take magnetic readings and record the weather. The team watched as the ship sailed away to the horizon before the pack ice closed around it.

CONFINED TO QUARTERS

There was much to be done, and time was short. Borchgrevink and a companion managed to climb to the

Sled dogs were first taken to Antarctica in 1895 by the Norwegian Carsten Borchgrevink and are still used there today (below). He used expert handlers from Lapland.

summit of Cape Adare, a peak of 3,670 feet (1,100 m), before the bitterly cold Antarctic winter confined the party to their hut for 75 days. It was deeply depressing, and to make this harder for them all, the geologist Nicolai Hanson fell ill and died.

When the penguins returned in the spring to seek their breeding grounds, the expedition explored and mapped the region of Victoria Land.

At long last the *Southern Cross* returned to pick them up. It took them around the coast where Borchgrevink, along with Lt. Colbeck and one of the

Kim Westerkov/Tony Stone Imgaes

WHALING

Whaling is a very old industry. As early as the 11th century, the people of Northern Spain would spot whales from the coast, row out in small boats, and drive their prey onto beaches, where they were harpooned and then killed.

Whales were a valuable catch both for their meat and for their blubber, which was boiled down for lamp oil. The only species docile enough to be caught from small boats were right whales. Right whales were pursued far and wide by ships from Britain, the Netherlands, and North America.

From the 18th century hunters turned their attention to the sperm whale, found in both southern and northern waters. This species contained spermaceti oil, which was useful for cosmetics and candles, and sometimes ambergris, used in perfume manufacture. American whalers risked their lives in the southern seas to capture these giants.

The rorquals, including the fin, humpback, and blue whales, were too big for traditional forms of whaling. They were not hunted until steamships and the harpoon gun were invented. A blue whale can grow to 100 feet (30 m) in length and weigh 100 tons. Harpooned, a blue whale is capable of dragging a steam whaler for half a day over a distance of 50 miles (80 km).

The Norwegians dominated whaling in the early 20th century, establishing whaling stations in the Antarctic from the early 1900s and bringing in factory ships from the 1920s. It was their early voyages that began to open up the south polar region to explorers.

Norwegian steam-powered whalers haul their catch back to a whaling station on Antarctica (right).

Hulton Getty

Left: Once on dry land, the whales would be "flensed"—stripped of their rich, blubbery skin. This would be turned into oil for fuel and lubricants. In the course of 100 years or so of whaling, the Southern Ocean's whale population has been reduced by 85 percent.

Hulton Getty

Finnish dog-handlers, pioneered the technique of sledding in Antarctica and reached latitude 78° 50' South: the farthest south anyone had ever been.

By the summer of 1900 Borchgrevink was back in England enjoying grudging recognition from those who had doubted his abilities. He made it quite clear that conquest of the Antarctic was possible. Indeed, within a year no fewer than five separate national expeditions, roughly coordinated, were setting out to follow in Borchgrevink's footsteps.

THE *BELGICA*

While the *Southern Cross* was nudging its way through the ice floes, another ship was experiencing its first Antarctic winter frozen in the pack ice. This was the extraordinary little bulldog of a vessel, the *Belgica*.

Formerly a Norwegian sealer, the ship was renamed by a Belgian naval officer, Adrien Comte de Gerlache de Gomery, who persuaded his government and scientific societies to back an Antarctic expedition. He had rehearsed polar survival techniques in Norway.

The adventures of the *Belgica* were recorded by the American explorer Frederick Cook, who had been in Greenland with Robert Peary in 1891. He had joined as the ship's doctor, having failed to raise his own expedition. Also on board was the Norwegian Roald Amundsen, enjoying his first taste of Antarctic travel and learning vital lessons about how to tackle the region.

The *Belgica* left Ostend, Belgium, in August 1897 and took five months to reach the Antarctic Circle. De Gerlache spent some time studying the peoples of Tierra del Fuego and neighboring islands. From the tip of South America he took his ship and crew of 19 men down into the Antarctic.

In January 1898 they made a series of landings and became the first men to camp overnight on the mainland. They were exceptionally lucky with the weather conditions, and de Gerlache was encouraged to explore farther along the coast. By now it was April, and winter was closing in. A fierce storm—which

The team that boarded the Belgica (above) in 1897 was not prepared for the rigors of a polar winter. Many of them suffered terribly from heart trouble, bad digestion, and poor circulation.

almost smashed the *Belgica* to matchwood—broke up the pack ice and enabled the ship to push even farther south, despite the misgivings of the crew. Then the inevitable happened: they were frozen in. In his ignorance De Gerlache believed the Antarctic winter would be milder than that in the Arctic. He would bitterly regret his mistake.

A CRUEL WINTER

The terrible Antarctic winter closed in for four sunless months. The isolation and the constantly howling wind drove some of the men crazy, although Cook did his best to revive their spirits. The party

Ben Osborne/Tony Stone Images

Popperfoto

Above: This serene dawn in Antarctica gives a false impression of what winter is like there: icy temperatures, howling winds, blizzards, and the darkness of endless night.

Captain Robert Falcon Scott (left) took the Discovery to Antarctica in 1901–1904. The expedition was well planned and proved to be a complete success. Scott also proved his worth as a leader of men.

hauled sleds on a few trips and climbed some ice ridges, but they could not get far. In the end they stayed on or next to their ship, held fast in the compacted ice, for 347 days.

When the summer came in November, they explored a little but then put their efforts into trying to free the *Belgica*; the prospect of another winter was too grisly to bear. They tried using explosives on the ice, but these merely blew a dent in the surface. Summer passed, and the icy autumn air returned.

Finally they hit on a desperate plan: to hack a channel through the ice. For two and a half grueling months they sawed through the ice until at last, on March 28, 1899, the *Belgica* broke free and steamed to the safety of South America.

OTHER PIONEERS

The pioneering exploits of Borchgrevink and de Gerlache were a great boost for further Antarctic exploration. The trips that followed in the early 1900s included a reconnaissance by Robert Scott, who sailed in the newly built steamer

Discovery with Ernest Shackleton and Edward Wilson, arriving in Antarctica in January 1902.

Another was led by the Scottish scientist William Bruce. He took the *Scotia*, a converted Norwegian whaler, on two separate voyages in 1903 and 1904. In the second of these Bruce managed to reach latitude 74° South in the Weddell Sea and chart new territory.

OTTO NORDENSKJÖLD

The most dramatic exploit was led by Otto Nordenskjöld, a young geologist and nephew of the man who had navigated the entire Northeast Passage in the Arctic. He sailed in the *Antarctic*, captained by Carl Larsen. Nordenskjöld and five companions were put ashore on Snow Hill Island for the winter, aiming to explore inland with dog teams. Larsen left them on February 12, 1902, intending to pick them up the next year.

At first all went well: the explorers made fascinating discoveries of life that existed there 100 million years ago and took their dog sleds hundreds of miles inland. When February came, they waited hopefully for the *Antarctic*, but it could not reach them through the thickening ice. To survive, they were forced to kill and eat 30 seals and more than 400 penguins.

They sat out their second winter engaged in research, and when spring came, Nordenskjöld and his colleague Ole Jonassen decided to sled inland.

The morning of October 12, 1903, witnessed the first of an incredible series of events. While traversing the coast of Vega Island, Nordenskjöld and Jonassen saw two dark dots against the ice, thinking them at first to be penguins.

A FATEFUL MEETING

But the figures came sledding toward them. They were two of a party of three the *Antarctic* had put onto the ice to search for Nordenskjöld when it became obvious that the ship would not reach the shore. However, the three rescuers could not cross the slushy seas, so they had

Antarctica (below) is made up of about five million square miles (more than 13 million square kilometers) of windswept ice and rock. Today 2,000–3,000 people live and work there, but in 1903 the continent was uninhabited. Getting lost or stranded would have spelled doom for most explorers—it was an amazing stroke of luck that the crew of the Antarctic *was rescued.*

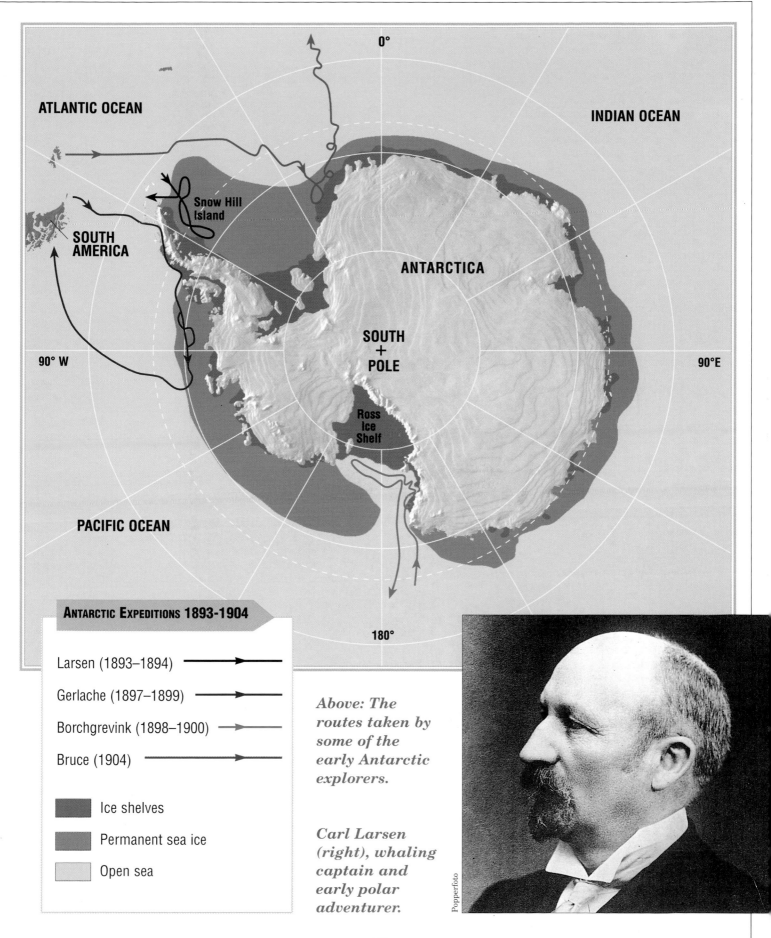

ATLANTIC OCEAN

INDIAN OCEAN

Snow Hill Island

SOUTH AMERICA

ANTARCTICA

SOUTH + POLE

Ross Ice Shelf

90° W

90°E

PACIFIC OCEAN

0°

180°

ANTARCTIC EXPEDITIONS 1893-1904

Larsen (1893–1894)

Gerlache (1897–1899)

Borchgrevink (1898–1900)

Bruce (1904)

Ice shelves

Permanent sea ice

Open sea

Above: The routes taken by some of the early Antarctic explorers.

Carl Larsen (right), whaling captain and early polar adventurer.

Popperfoto

Popperfoto

Jean-Baptiste Charcot (left), sent to rescue Nordenskjöld, spent five years charting the Antarctic coast.

The ecstatic meeting (below) between the crew of the Uruguay and Nordenskjöld was portrayed on a French magazine cover of the day.

to leave Antarctica. Had it been a day later, they would all have been stranded and would almost certainly have died.

RESCUER MAKES MAPS INSTEAD

When Nordenskjöld was reported missing, a French party, led by Jean-Baptiste Charcot, an oceanographer and doctor, set out in the *Français* to find them. When Charcot arrived to find that they had been saved, he set about exploring the coast instead and mapped a great deal of new territory.

Scott, too, was reported missing, and expeditions were sent to find him; but he returned triumphantly in 1904 to excite audiences with his accounts of his sled-hauling inland. The stage was set for an assault on the geographic South Pole.

built a crude stone hut and sat out the winter. They had set out again at the end of September, and it was only by the most astonishing good luck that they had met up with Nordenskjöld.

Now united, Nordenskjöld's team and the rescue party waited in their camp for the *Antarctic*. At last, on November 8 a mast appeared. This, unexpectedly, turned out to be an Argentinian naval ship, the *Uruguay*. With no clue as to the whereabouts of the *Antarctic*, the Norwegians packed up and prepared to leave with the Argentinians.

THE DOGS BEGIN TO BARK

That very night the dogs began to bark excitedly. One of the party went out to quiet them and saw a group of men. They turned out to be the crew of the *Antarctic,* which had foundered in the ice in February 25 miles (40 km) from land. With sleds and boats the crew had made for shore. There they had spent the winter in a hut and had killed 1,100 penguins for food. It was a miraculous stroke of luck that they found Nordenskjöld on the very day he was due

AKG, London

ICEBREAKERS—HEAVYWEIGHT CRUSHERS OF THE POLAR SEAS

Images Colour Library

The first ships designed to break through ice were used on rivers to clear the way for shipping in winter. One of the earliest examples was a steam tug used on the Delaware River from 1837. However, these river icebreakers were not strong enough to be used in polar regions. Thick polar ice is particularly tough and cannot be smashed by a ramming action.

A Russian naval officer, who had studied the famous *Fram* designed for Fridtjof Nansen, invented the first real Arctic icebreaker. He was Sepan Osipovich Makarov, whose ship *Yermak* was launched in 1898. Makarov knew that although sea ice cannot easily be rammed, it can be attacked from above. So the *Yermak* was designed to ride up on the frozen surface until the downward pressure of its steel bows cracked the ice. In this way a channel could eventually be cut.

Above: The Russian icebreaker Yamal *carves a route through the thick ice of the Arctic Ocean, just one degree south of the North Pole.*

Modern icebreakers are immensely powerful but are still in danger of being "hung up" on extremely thick ice. In such a situation special tanks in the hull pump out oil and water to destabilize the ship and rock it back into the water. On older icebreakers the entire crew would run back and forth across the decks to rock the ship—a maneuver known as "sallying."

The first ship ever to crash right through the pack ice to the North Pole was the Soviet icebreaker *Arktika*, which made its historic voyage in 1977. Its mighty engines were powered by nuclear turbines producing 75,000 horsepower.

THE RACE FOR THE SOUTH POLE

Captain Robert Scott's first expedition to Antarctica, which ended in 1904, was greeted as a tremendous success. He brought back valuable data about the rocks and meager vegetation of the South Polar region. And to crown it all, Scott—with Edward Wilson and Ernest Shackleton—had ventured farther south, hauling their sleds, than anyone before: to latitude 82° 17' South.

This was a heroic feat, for the going was unimaginably tough in Antarctica. The terrain rises toward the Pole to the highest plateau on earth, with altitudes of over 11,000 feet (3,350 m), and the ice and snow are always treacherous. Any exertion at these altitudes is exhausting: the cold is intense, and breathing in the thin air demands severe effort.

Shackleton had particular problems. A lively and playful Irishman, he was immensely strong—and a risk taker who

Above: The winter quarters of Robert Scott's Discovery *expedition of 1901–1904. The ship broke free from the ice and sailed for home on February 16, 1904.*

Popperfoto

Popperfoto

had cut his teeth as an adventurous merchant seaman. Yet it was he who suffered most on this first long trip into the cold interior. Stricken by scurvy, he could not help haul the sled back to base. The three explorers spent 90 days on their trek in 1903, and they barely survived.

Explorers from the Discovery *(left to right), Shackleton, Scott, and Wilson pose by their sleds.*

THE AGONY OF FROSTBITE

Of all the hardships endured by polar explorers, frostbite ranks among the most unpleasant and painful. This condition can occur when the outside temperature falls below 32°F (0°C).

The first parts of the body to suffer are usually the toes and fingers. Frostbite sets in when the living tissue freezes. The ice particles kill the tissue, leading eventually to gangrene (rotting of the flesh). In the 18th and early 19th centuries it was almost impossible to treat frostbite with any measure of success. This meant that many explorers exposed to the cold for long periods lost fingers and toes—or even their lives—to this agonizing affliction.

Shackleton was in such bad shape on his return to base in 1904 that Scott sent him home. Scott himself stayed on until 1905. After several relief expeditions had been sent to rescue him—though he thought he was in no trouble—he took his ship, the *Discovery*, back to England.

Although Jean-Baptiste Charcot was still charting the coast, Scott's return signaled a brief lull in Antarctic exploration. The Norwegian Roald Amundsen was planning to beat the Americans to the more accessible North Pole, and Scott took up a new post in the British navy. His team of explorers returned to their careers, and the *Discovery* was sold. Although the International Geographical Congress of 1904 urged more expeditions to Antarctica, no one was yet prepared to back such a trip.

SHACKLETON'S AMBITIONS
Despite the severe health problems suffered on his last trip, Shackleton had not given up the idea of conquering the South

EQUIPPING A POLAR EXPEDITION

Shackleton placed great importance on getting the right clothing and equipment for the trip of 1907–1909, basing his selection on his experience on the *Discovery* expedition. He used reindeer-skin sleeping bags, some of which were large enough for three men to sleep in together for extra warmth. Special boots called *finnesko*, made from reindeer leg skin, were shipped over from Lapland, plus others made from head skin. On a visit to Norway he ordered 30 sleds based on a pattern designed by Fridtjof Nansen, as well as ski equipment and mittens made from wolf and dog skin.

Below: The camp set up by Shackleton (inset) at Back Door Bay on Ross Island. The stores were hauled to land by ponies with just hours to spare before the ice broke up.

Pole. Unfortunately he had no means of raising an expedition. He tried to join the British navy but was turned down. He worked for a while on a popular magazine, then left to become secretary of the Royal Scottish Geographical Society. He even tried to get elected to the British Parliament—but failed.

However, his bid to enter politics introduced him to a wealthy industrialist, William Beardmore, who agreed to provide funds of £7,000—a huge sum in those days—for an attempt on the geographic South Pole. That would be the first goal. The second would be to reach the magnetic South Pole.

PLANNING AND PREPARATION

In April 1907 Shackleton announced his plans in the London *Times* newspaper. He advertised for men to join him and for financial support; not surprisingly there were plenty of volunteers. These included army officers and scientists such as the Australian physicist Douglas Mawson, who was to become one of the great names in Antarctic exploration.

Shackleton acquired a Norwegian sealing vessel, renamed the *Nimrod*, then addressed the difficult question of sled-hauling. The Norwegians urged him to take dogs, but he decided to use Siberian ponies. Scott had tried to use dog teams on the *Discovery* expedition, but with little success. Dog-handling required a lot of practice, and Scott's packs had fought viciously, tangling their har-

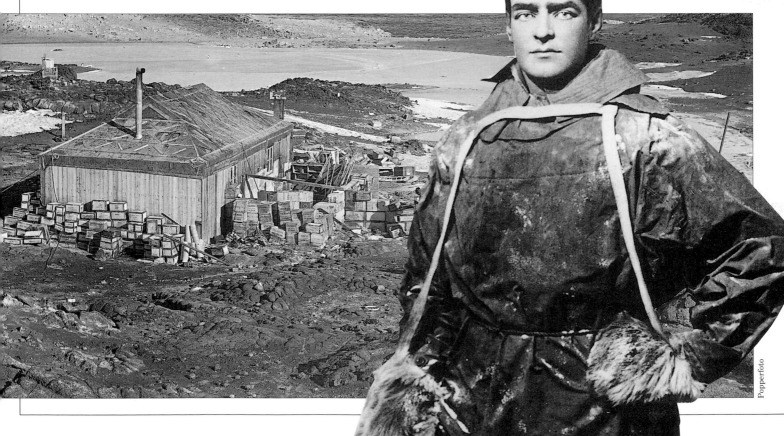

Popperfoto

Popperfoto

nesses. In the end, Shackleton did take a few dogs for local sledding trips, as well as two automobiles with skis fitted.

SOUTH AT LAST!

The *Nimrod* sailed from England on August 7, 1907. The ship was overloaded, and several ponies had to be left behind when the ship set out for the Antarctic from New Zealand on January 1, 1908.

Once through the pack ice, Shackleton moored in Back Door Bay on Ross Island—about 20 miles (32 km) from the original *Discovery* hut. Before winter set in, a party climbed the volcano Mount Erebus. The team then spent the dark months preparing for the twin assaults: Doug Mawson would attempt the magnetic Pole, while Shackleton would head for the geographic Pole.

In October 1908 they began setting up forward depots with food supplies—by now standard practice in polar exploration. Then on November 6 Shackleton and three others began their journey into the unknown. It was not long before one pony was too weak to continue and was killed and eaten.

Their last pony disappeared into a crevass and, with it, vital food supplies.

By November 26 they had reached farther than Scott had done, but only three ponies remained. Within a week they had killed two of them. The explorers were now thousands of feet up, and breathing

Shackleton took the Nimrod *(above) into McMurdo Sound in 1907. This annoyed Scott, who had asked, a little unreasonably, for exclusive use of the area after his* Discovery *expedition made a landing there in 1902. Shackleton used the Sound only because it offered a safe mooring.*

was laborious. Their last pony disappeared into a crevass and, with it, vital food supplies.

By Christmas Day 1908 they were at 9,500 feet (2,900 m) altitude, on the glacier leading to the central Antarctic plateau—just 250 miles (400 km) from the South Pole. Hauling their sleds themselves, they made only a few miles a day.

Finally, on January 9 at 11,000 feet (3,350 m), with little food left, and all of them suffering with severe headaches from the altitude and glaring snow, Shackleton reluctantly turned back. They had marched to within 97 miles (155 km) of their prize. It was an outstanding achievement, and they had shown the way for others.

When Shackleton's party staggered back to the camp, they learned that there had been a success: Mawson had reached the magnetic South Pole on January 16, 1908, and a third expedition had explored a wide sweep of the mainland. All in all, it was a triumph for Shackleton's flair and determination.

SHACKLETON AND THE *JAMES CAIRD*

Even after the South Pole had been reached, Shackleton refused to abandon his Antarctic ambitions. On August 8, 1914, he set out again, intending to make the first land crossing of Antarctica. But his expedition never really got started. After sailing from South Georgia his ship, the *Endurance*, was crushed in the ice and sank, leaving the expedition stranded (① on the map). As the ship went down, the party salvaged some provisions and the ship's small open whaling boats. Camping on the ice, they were gradually carried farther north. When the pack ice melted, they took to the boats.

They drifted along, taking their loaded boats between huge icebergs while orca whales bumped them inquisitively. In April 1916, they reached Elephant Island ②. There they killed an elephant seal, which fed them and provided oil for a fire.

Leaving 22 men camped on Elephant Island, Shackleton and five others decided to sail 800 miles (1,300 km) through stormy seas in an attempt to seek rescue for the whole party. They used one of the longboats, the *James Caird*, which they reinforced and half-decked. The terrible journey in the 22-ft (6.7-m) boat ③ took them from April 23 to May 10, 1916.

They were washed ashore in a remote bay on South Georgia ④, where they converted the boat into a crude shelter. Shackleton then climbed a 6,000-ft (1,800-m) cliff and struggled over rugged terrain,

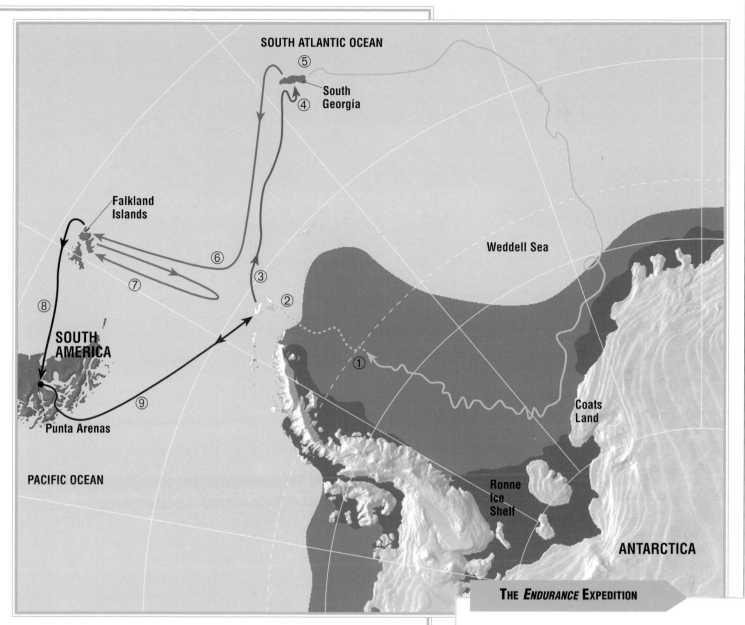

SOUTH ATLANTIC OCEAN

⑤

South
④ Georgia

Falkland
Islands

Weddell Sea

⑥

⑦ ③

② ②

⑧

SOUTH
AMERICA ①

⑨ Coats
Land

Punta Arenas

PACIFIC OCEAN

Ronne
Ice
Shelf

ANTARCTICA

THE *ENDURANCE* EXPEDITION

Route of the *Endurance*

Route to Elephant Island

Route of the *James Caird*
to South Georgia

Attempted rescue routes

Shackleton to Punta Arenas

Final rescue route

with practically no protection or equipment, to seek help at the whaling station at Stromness Bay ⑤. He had made the first land crossing of South Georgia Island.

Shackleton chartered a ship and made an attempt to reach the rest of his party ⑥ but was driven back by pack ice and had to retreat to the Falkland Islands. Another attempt in a Uruguayan trawler also failed ⑦. Finally, Shackleton sailed to Punta Arenas ⑧. Here the Chilean authorities provided him with a ship that reached Elephant Island in August 1916 and rescued all 22 men ⑨.

The map above shows the routes taken by the Endurance, *the* James Caird, *and Shackleton's rescue attempts. Left, the men of the* Endurance *drag the longboat, the* James Caird, *over the ice.*

The **Nimrod** *expedition of 1908 (above) nearly reached the Pole and set the pace for the final attempts by Scott and Amundsen. Scott was later to follow much of the route mapped out by Shackleton.*

It so happened that the news of Shackleton's near-conquest of the South Pole broke just as Frederick Cook and Robert Peary both claimed to have reached the North Pole in the spring of 1909. Suddenly there now remained only one great prize in exploration: the geographic South Pole. Two men in particular—both experienced, both tough—were very eager to claim it: Roald Amundsen and Robert Scott.

BRITISH BACKING

While waiting for news of Shackleton, Scott had landed an office job at the British Admiralty. He was quietly planning another attempt to reach the Pole and was testing motorized caterpillar-tracked vehicles—a newfangled idea in those days.

Scott announced his plans in September 1909, touring the country and lecturing in order to raise public support. The British government contributed funds, as did the Royal Geographical Society. Scott picked a team, which included Dr. Edward Wilson from the earlier *Discovery* expedition, and fitted out a Scottish whaling ship that he renamed the *Terra Nova*.

Scott sailed from London on June 1, 1910, and reached Melbourne, Australia, that October. There he was handed a cable from Amundsen that read simply: "Beg leave to inform you proceeding Antarctica." It was a shock and the first realization that a race was on against a formidable opponent.

> *Suddenly there now remained only one great prize in exploration: the geographic South Pole.*

Amundsen had made a swift change of plan. He had acquired Fridtjof Nansen's ship, the *Fram*, and had intended to drift in the pack ice toward the North Pole.

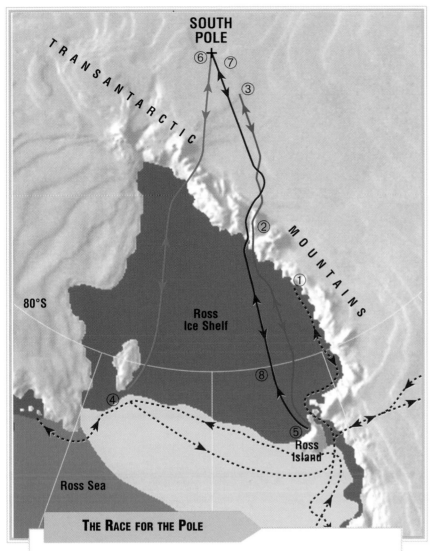

THE RACE FOR THE POLE

Scott (1901–1904) ‑ ‑ ‑ ‑ ‑ ‑ ‑ ‑ ‑ ‑ ‑ ‑ →

Shackleton (1907–1909) ———————→

Amundsen (1910–1912) ———————→

Scott (1911–1912) ———————→

▨ Ice shelf

① Scott's farthest point, December 1901
② Shackleton climbs Beardmore Glacier, December 1908
③ Shackleton's farthest point, January 1909
④ Amundsen's starting point, October 1911
⑤ Scott leaves base camp, October 1911
⑥ Amundsen reaches Pole, December 1911
⑦ Scott reaches Pole, January 1912
⑧ Scott's last camp, March 1912

After setting sail, however, he heard that Peary had beaten him to the Pole. There and then he decided to make an attempt on the South Pole. He turned south and cabled Scott from the island of Madeira.

NORWEGIAN KNOW-HOW

Amundsen was equipped in what had become the classic Norwegian polar style. He had 97 dogs from Greenland, where they were accustomed to tough Arctic conditions. He took only 19 men and intended to travel light. Amundsen was single-minded, coldly practical, and confident in pursuit of his goal.

Scott was a total contrast. Full of pride and prejudice, the British naval officer was reluctant to admit that his main intention was to race for the Pole. Fatally, he believed that it was more noble for men and ponies to haul sleds

Skiing and sled-hauling rapidly brought Scott (above) and his men out in a sweat, despite the cold.

Hulton Getty

Above: Scott's ship the Terra Nova *at its moorings in the Ross Sea. Banks of thick fog, huge, drifting icebergs, and the instability of the pack ice were a constant worry for the ship's crew.*

than to use lowly dogs. He took a few dogs but relied mainly on Siberian ponies and caterpillar-tracked motor vehicles.

Looking back, it is easy to see that this grueling race could only have been won by sled dogs and Norwegian know-how. Shackleton suspected as much when he heard of the Norwegian's challenge and discovered that Scott was following his own route across the Antarctic plateau.

The lessons learned in the Arctic—by Charles Hall, Fridtjof Nansen, Robert Peary, and others—seemed to count for nothing in Scott's opinion, and his choice of animals probably sealed his fate.

A LATE DEPARTURE

Scott was off the mainland by January 1911 and began to prepare his base. Very soon, however, several ponies fell

through the ice and perished, and he lost a caterpillar vehicle. As before, he could not control the dogs he had taken.

Some of his party out exploring eastward from Hut Point came across Amundsen's *Fram*. They saw that the Norwegian had a head start: he would already be 60 miles (100 km) nearer the Pole. This was predictable: Scott's ponies were delayed because they could not deal so well with the terrain.

There were a number of other key differences between the two expeditions. Whereas the Norwegians were all together on an equal footing, Scott maintained a clear distinction between officers and men. Also, the Norwegians traveled light, while Scott's party was weighed down with masses of bulky scientific equipment.

Amundsen set off on October 19. His well-fed and disciplined huskies whisked him over the ice—four teams, 42 dogs in all. His teams had a tough time sled-hauling up onto the glacier that led to the plateau, but once they were there, the going was easier.

It was then they carried out their preplanned masterstroke: the massacre of more than half their dogs. They shot 24 to provide food for themselves and the other dogs at a point they named "The Butcher's Shop." Amundsen confessed in his diaries that he hated doing this, but it was essential for their survival.

After being snowed in by a blizzard, they struggled over some unstable terrain. Then the weather cleared, and they skimmed along at 20 miles (32 km) a day. By December 8 they had passed Shackleton's farthest point.

Amundsen spent three days at the Pole, checking data and planting flags.

At last, on December 14, 1911, their instruments told them they were at the South Pole—more or less. They planted the Norwegian flag triumphantly at 3:00 P.M. Amundsen admitted that he was not exactly sure where the Pole was because his readings could not be that accurate, and so they marked out a circle with a radius of 12 miles (19 km) that would definitely encompass the Pole.

THREE DAYS AT THE POLE
Amundsen spent three days at the Pole, checking readings and planting more flags. He left messages for Scott, who he knew was perilously delayed. Then, to avoid the glare of the sun, Amundsen traveled back mainly at night. He reached the *Fram* by January 25 and a week later set sail for home.

ICEBERGS OF ANTARCTICA

The Ross Ice Shelf, from which Scott and Amundsen launched their South Pole expeditions, is a vast sheet of frozen freshwater produced by snowfall on the mainland. The snow collects and then creeps very slowly along glaciers (rivers of ice). When the glaciers reach the coast, they keep on creeping out to sea like a huge tongue. Eventually, pieces break off the tip of the "tongue" and drift away as icebergs. The icebergs range in size from "growlers" as small as a piano to blocks as large as a small country. The largest iceberg ever known measured 206 miles (333 km) long. Because they are made from the collected snowfall of many winters, icebergs can be several thousand years old.

Scott had set off on October 23—four days later than his rival. Before his party was out of sight of their camp, their motor vehicles broke down and had to be left behind. They followed Shackleton's route and kept pace with his journey times, but by December they had shot all their ponies. The dogs took them a little further before they resorted to man-hauling the sleds. When they were 170 miles (272 km) from their goal, Scott sent the support party back. He continued

Below: Amundsen took plenty of readings at the South Pole to make sure of his exact location. He also left a note for Scott, in case he did not make it back alive.

Hulton Getty

61

Sled Dogs

The uneven surface of the polar regions makes any form of transportation very difficult. A great deal of polar exploration was carried out with the help of husky dogs drawing sleds.

Ponies, as used by Scott and others, were rarely successful: they could not cope with the worst conditions, and their bulky hay feed had to be carried on the sleds along with all the other equipment. Dogs, by contrast, could put up with the very worst winter conditions. And as a last resort, they could be killed to feed both the remaining animals and their human masters.

Wolflike husky dogs (below) had been used in Greenland and Siberia by Eskimos and other northern peoples since earliest times. The Norwegians were among the first to adopt them for polar expeditions and to learn the specialized art of handling them. This is one reason why Fridtjof Nansen and Roald Amundsen achieved such success.

Sled design itself evolved over years of exploration. The Eskimos used frozen fish, rather than wood, for runners. Nansen's lightweight design had skilike runners on a structure that was lashed together so that it was pliable and would snake over rough ground.

with four men: Bowers, Evans, Oates, and Wilson. Their diaries give us a clear account of their ill-fated journey.

An awful place

As they approached the Pole on January 17, they saw Amundsen's tracks. Bitterly disappointed, they pressed on in a force 4 to 6 gale. It was, in Wilson's words, "the coldest march I ever remember." At the Pole they found Amundsen's tent, topped by the Norwegian flag, abandoned a month earlier.

It was a cruel blow to all their hopes. They camped overnight. The wind was blowing hard, and it was unbelievably cold. Scott wrote in his diary, "Great God, this is an awful place." After making some meteorological observations, they headed back.

At first the wind was with them and progress was good. But frostbite and snow blindness began to take their toll, and Evans was troubled by a cut hand.

John Beatty/Tony Stone Images

Popperfoto

For the last 10 days of March Scott, Wilson, and Bowers were confined to their tent by a terrible blizzard. Weakened by the intense cold, and starving, they lay down and waited for death. Scott wrote to the families of his companions to tell them of their bravery; Oates had walked out of the tent to die so that the others might continue. The last entries in his diary describe their end.

"March 22–23: Blizzard bad as ever— Wilson and Bowers unable to start . . . must be near the end.

"Thursday, March 29: Continuous gale . . . I do not think we can hope for better things now. We shall stick it out to the end, but we are getting weaker, of course, and the end cannot be far.

"It seems a pity, but I do not think I can write more.

R. Scott

"Last entry. For God's sake, look after our people."

By February the weather had become atrocious, and food was now strictly rationed. Evans was struggling to keep up, and Oates had a painful foot.

They plodded on wretchedly, making slow progress, through ever-worsening visibility. Evans finally fell behind on February 17; they found him kneeling in the snow, stupefied by cold. He died a few hours later. The others pressed on, now only 250 miles (400 km) from One Ton Depot, their nearest supply depot.

When Scott's party reached the South Pole, they found Amundsen's tent (above). Their intense disappointment at Amundsen's triumph is plain to see on their faces (below).

They died on or about March 31, only 11 miles (18 km) from One Ton Depot. Their bodies were found eight months later.

As he stepped out into the blizzard, Oates turned and said, "I may be some time."

Oates's foot grew steadily worse. Finally, while they were camped in mid-March in temperatures of –40°F (–40°C), he took off his boot and showed them the swollen, blackened foot. Should he go on? he asked the others. Of course, insisted Scott. But three days later, in the midst of a blizzard, Oates stood and announced, "I am just going outside, and I may be some time." He never came back.

Popperfoto

MAPPING
THE
ANTARCTIC

At the time Amundsen reached the South Pole in 1911, the geography of the vast Antarctic continent was still not fully understood. It was difficult to map the coast from the sea or to distinguish between islands and mainland. Piecing together this immense mass of rock and creeping ice was a mapping nightmare of epic proportions.

A BRIDGE BETWEEN THE SEAS?

One question taxing geographers was whether a strip of land existed between the two great ice shelves, one in the Weddell Sea and the other in the Ross Sea, or whether they were simply connected by ice. If the latter were true, then Antarctica would in effect consist of two huge land masses.

Wilhelm Filchner, an army officer and geophysicist, set out with a German expedition in 1911–1912 to solve this mystery. By February 1912 his ship, the *Deutschland*, had penetrated farther into the Weddell Sea ice than anyone before.

But the dangers of exploration were brought home to him as they were seeking a site for a base on the ice shelf. A bay was spotted, and so they drew in and unloaded dogs, ponies, and stores and began to build their huts on the ice. They had nearly finished the work when there was a deafening roar. A huge section of ice broke away and bobbed in the sea, creating a swell that threatened to engulf them. They retreated to the *Deutschland* just in time and waited for the sea to calm. When they tried to find their ice bay again, it had disappeared.

Filchner's expedition made little headway toward its main aim, and it was not until the 1950s that scientists, taking soundings in the ice, established the true situation. A strip of land only 700 miles (1,120 km) wide separates the two great ice shelves, although from the air they seem to be much farther apart.

AERIAL SURVEYS

In an effort to get a perspective on the puzzling coast of Antarctica, one or two explorers had taken to the air. On the

Popperfoto

Wilhelm Filchner (above) set out to discover whether the Weddell Sea (below) was connected to the Ross Sea by dry land or simply by ice alone. But his expedition was almost swallowed up by treacherous ice.

John Beatty/Tony Stone Images

first *Discovery* expedition Scott floated in a balloon to 1,500 feet (500 m) in a small basket safely tethered by a rope.

It was not until the 1920s, however, that explorers began to use aircraft to piece together the geography of the Antarctic. The first-ever Antarctic flights were made by Hubert Wilkins, the Australian who was the first to fly across the Arctic from west to east in 1928. In the same year Wilkins also flew over Palmer Land in the Antarctic.

RICHARD BYRD

In the pioneering work of polar flights, however, one man stands out as the greatest of all explorer-aviators: Richard Byrd, the American who had been the first to fly over the North Pole in 1926. With advice from Amundsen, generous backing from Rockefeller and Edsel Ford, and help with equipment from the U.S. Navy, Byrd raised in 1927 an enormous expedition by the standards of the time. He and his party of scientists had two ships: a converted sealer and a freighter that he renamed after his mother—the *Eleanor Bolling*.

The ships sailed from New Zealand in the summer of 1928, weighed down with provisions that might prevent the need to eat too many penguins—including 1,200 lbs. (544 kg) of cookies. Byrd took three airplanes adapted for the cold conditions; they needed vast amounts of fuel.

LITTLE AMERICA

Byrd prepared well and sought advice, which included a plea from Amundsen to take dog teams. As it turned out, the 95 huskies in Byrd's party were invaluable in the process of setting up camps and for making short forays.

Byrd found a landing site near the Bay of Whales that looked suitable for an airstrip and set up "Little America," the most elaborate camp ever to grace Antarctica. From there Byrd made his

Jim Corwin/Corbis

Over the years almost every method of transportation, including the hot-air balloon (above), has been used in a bid to cross Antarctica's inhospitable terrain.

first flight on January 15, 1929. He was in grave danger of getting lost because he was so close to the magnetic pole that his compass would not work, and there was a blinding glare from the ice. But that first one-hour flight was, by Byrd's own account, spectacular. It allowed him to survey hundreds of square miles and to take photographs for later analysis that would in an instant show the true shape of the continent.

Two weeks later Byrd went up again when the weather cleared. Flying low, he saw ahead a range of mountains that explorers on the ground had missed. He named them the Rockefeller Mountains after his sponsor, and sent out a team of geologists in a plane to study the peaks.

Nothing was heard of the team for a few days. Finally, they radioed to say that they were caught in a blizzard and were waiting for clear weather. At length, Byrd and his pilot Smith went

In a series of expeditions (below) dating from 1929, Byrd (right) did much to extend the mapping of Antarctica.

Hulton Getty

BYRD'S ANTARCTIC EXPEDITIONS

First expedition, 1929–1930

Air reconnaissance and survey routes - - - ▶ - - - - - - - -

Flight to South Pole ───────▶

Second expedition, 1934–1935

Land survey routes ───────▶

Air survey routes ───────▶

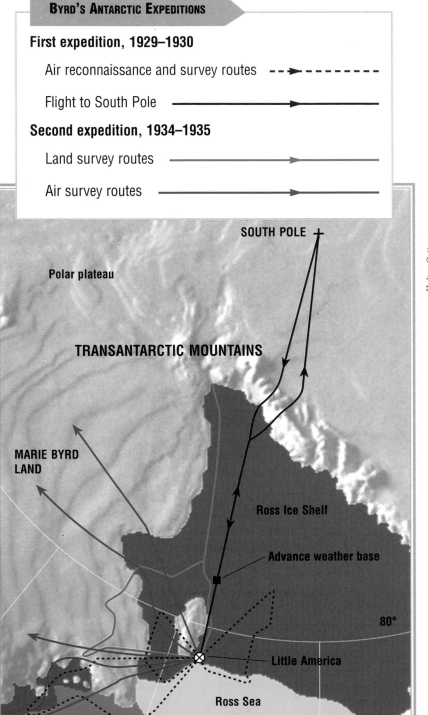

SOUTH POLE ✛

Polar plateau

TRANSANTARCTIC MOUNTAINS

MARIE BYRD LAND

Ross Ice Shelf

Advance weather base

80°

Little America

Ross Sea

looking for the geologists, flying blind through the clouds and snow. It was getting late when they caught sight of the mountains. But there was no sign of their party, and they were about to turn back when the pilot spotted a column of smoke. And as the plane rocked in the strong wind, they saw a landing place marked out for them, where they made a nerve-racking touchdown.

The three geologists had a terrifying tale to tell. Although they had tethered their airplane when a storm broke, the hurricane winds were too strong. The plane had been ripped from the ground and blown along like paper for half a mile (0.8 km), spinning in the air before it crashed and broke up on a mountainside.

A LONG, COLD WINTER

Byrd took the geologists back to Little America. There the party settled down to wait out the worst of the winter weather, with the planes safely stored in "igloo" hangars. The Antarctic summer came slowly. On September 1, when New York was burning in temperatures of 94°F (34°C), Little America was frozen in at –63°F (–52°C), and it was October before Byrd could begin preparations for his attempted flight over the South Pole.

Byrd's first attempt did not succeed due to a fuel leak, but he learned many valuable lessons. A heavy fuel payload, and the need to take aerial photography, restricted his plane to an altitude of 11,000 feet (3,350 m)—but he would need to overfly the Maud mountains, with their peaks of up to 13,000 feet (3,960 m).

On November 28 Byrd and his crew—pilot, navigator, radio operator, and photographer—were told by an advance party that the weather was right. They

Below: The cutter Bear arriving in the Antarctic ice. This was the ship that carried Richard Byrd, as well as 74 colleagues and three aircraft, to Antarctica in 1928. After his historic flight the following year Byrd became the first man ever to have flown over both Poles.

took off once again to head directly for the South Pole in one long hop. All went well until they reached the Maud range. Then Byrd had to take a tremendous risk. There was only enough fuel for a single flight through the mountains. So he headed for a glacial valley.

A NERVE-WRACKING FLIGHT
It was a nerve-wracking flight. The wind over the Liv Glacier buffeted the small plane like a leaf as they shuddered along at just over 9,000 feet (2,740 m). To gain height they had to lose some weight.

Should they jettison fuel or their food supplies—which would be needed if they crashlanded? Bravely, they chose to risk starvation, heaving out first one 200-lbs. (90-kg) food bag and then another. Luckily, the plane bobbed up and carried

Hulton Getty

them narrowly over the ridge at the end of the glacier. They reached the South Pole 12 hours after takeoff, at 1:14 A.M. on the morning of November 29. They circled it, the photographer McKinley clicking away madly, to bring back an astonishing record of a land that few footsteps had ever disturbed.

Byrd's historic flight was, in its way, every bit as daring as the expeditions over land of Amundsen and Scott. And as a means of surveying the millions of square miles of Antarctica it proved to be vastly superior. For the flight from Little America to the South Pole and back took only 16 hours, whereas the dog sleds of Amundsen had taken three months.

A GRIM WINTER ALONE

Byrd later led another expedition to Antarctica, from 1933 to 1935, making more surveys by land and air. He set up an Advance Weather Station about 120 miles (190 km) south of Little America, where he spent a grim winter alone recording meteorological observations. His air survey in late 1935 established that there was no sea channel between the Ross and Weddell Seas, so proving that Antactica was a single continent.

Hulton Getty

Ellsworth made the first trans-Antarctic flight in 1935. He returned in 1938–1939 with a small float plane (above), approaching from the Indian Ocean, to chart the area east of the Ross Sea.

After the conquest of the South Pole by air in 1929 the next target was a flight across the continent. There were, by then, veterans of polar air exploration prepared to fly crisscross over Antarctica, mapping and photographing it.

LINCOLN ELLSWORTH

One such man was the wealthy American Lincoln Ellsworth; he and Roald Amundsen had flown in the *Norge* airship across the Arctic in 1926. Ellsworth teamed up with the Australian

Left: The polar landscape seen from the air is awe inspiring. Early polar aviators were able to map vast areas with comparative ease by taking a series of aerial photographs that could be put together to give a complete picture of the terrain.

Galen Rowell/Corbis

Hubert Wilkins (who had been the first to fly across the Arctic from west to east).

Ellsworth and Wilkins were carrying on the work of Filchner, who had surveyed the area between the Ross and Weddell Seas. However, their 1933 expedition had to be abandoned because their aircraft was damaged, and the following year they were foiled by engine trouble.

ACROSS THE ANTARCTIC BY AIR

It was not until November 20, 1935, that Lincoln Ellsworth took off in his airplane the *Polar Star* to make a 2,200 mile (3,520 km) flight from an island in the Weddell Sea to the Ross Sea. His plane had to make four landings in appalling weather and eventually ran out of fuel just 15 miles (24 km) from Byrd's Little America. Ellsworth and his pilot walked the final distance to shelter.

DOUGLAS MAWSON

Among the other great polar aviators in the 1930s was the Australian Douglas Mawson. He had been in the first team to reach the magnetic South Pole in Shackleton's expedition of 1907–1909. Mawson led the 1929-1931 joint British, Australian, and New Zealand expedition in which large new areas of Antarctica were mapped from the air.

This was not, however, the end of overland exploration in the Antarctic. Indeed, the greatest gains were often made when sled teams and aircraft worked together, and this naturally became the standard pattern for research programs in the region.

Where Byrd, with Amundsen's advice, had shown the way, others like the British Graham Land Expedition of 1934–1937 established the technique. They followed up

INTERNATIONAL GEOPHYSICAL YEAR

In the uneasy peace that followed the Second World War there was a huge leap forward in scientific research in Antarctica. The driving force for this research came from the International Geophysical Year (IGY) of 1957–1958.

More than 60 nations, including both the United States and the Soviet Union, showed an interest in studying Antarctica during the 1950s. Plans were drawn up, and on July 1, 1957, IGY was launched. Twelve nations set up more than 50 permanent research stations on Antarctica or nearby islands. Equipment was brought over in huge cargo airplanes and was then distributed by droves of caterpillar-tracked vehicles.

Subjects for research included cosmic rays, glaciers, weather patterns, and gravity, among several others. For a year and a half the nations laid aside their political differences and pooled their resources. In one of the largest research programs ever seen, scientists amassed an extraordinary body of information that was made available to governments of every nation.

The success of IGY was preserved in the Antarctic Treaty, signed in Washington, D.C. in 1959. This landmark document, signed by 12 nations, ensured that Antarctic research would continue to be peaceful and cooperative, and that the continent would not be used for waste disposal or nuclear programs.

Below: This scene at the South Pole symbolizes the cooperative and international nature of Antarctic research, which was established largely through the success of IGY.

Morton Beebe/Corbis

reconnaissance flights with long overland sled journeys. By pooling their results, they corrected some earlier discovery claims—that what was originally thought to be mainland was in fact island, what had been called islands were peninsulas, and so forth.

INTERNATIONAL INTERESTS

With the Second World War came a new phase in Antarctic history. The explorers had, by and large, had their day, and the icebound continent began to witness the growth of international claims.

Many of these had strategic military and economic purposes. The United States established submarine tracking bases and after the war launched a series of expeditions. The greatest of these was Operation Highjump in 1946. It involved 4,500 men, 19 aircraft, 13 helicopters, and 13 U.S. Navy ships. It was one of a number of operations masterminded by

Byrd, who by then had exchanged hair-raising exploits for an admiral's pay.

In addition to the United States, several nations laid claim to Antarctic regions, including Argentina, Australia, Chile, and France. National bases were set up for scientific research. And in 1957 the United States established a permanently manned outpost at the Pole, naming it the Amundsen-Scott base in honor of its discoverers.

FUCHS AND HILLARY

In 1957-1958 the British Common-wealth TransAntarctic Expedition crossed Antarctica in relative style, using modern technology. The New Zealander Sir Edmund Hillary set up the depots along the route, and Britain's Sir Vivian Fuchs made the journey with snow tractors. With aircraft to scout out the land ahead and drop supplies—restocked by tractor and sled—this was more like a

Below: In 1957 the United States set up a permanently manned research and meteorological station at the South Pole, naming it the Amundsen-Scott base in honor of the pioneer explorers who first reached the spot.

THE UNITED STATES OF AMERICA
WELCOMES YOU TO
AMUNDSEN - SCOTT SOUTH POLE STATION

Images Colour Library

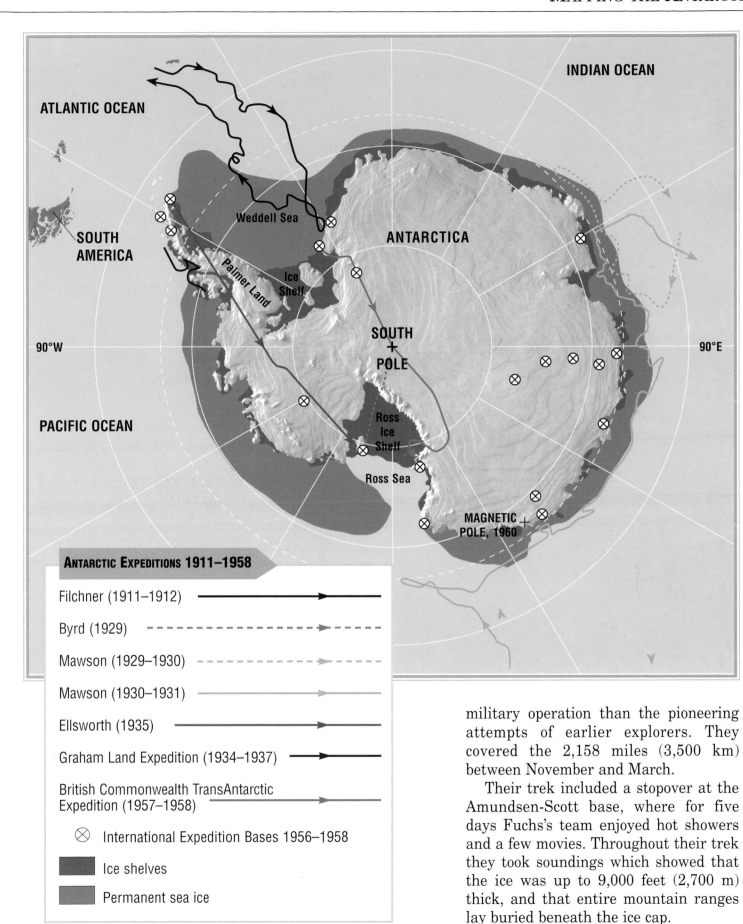

ATLANTIC OCEAN

INDIAN OCEAN

SOUTH
AMERICA

Weddell Sea

ANTARCTICA

Palmer Land

Ice
Shelf

90°W

SOUTH
+
POLE

90°E

PACIFIC OCEAN

Ross
Ice
Shelf

Ross Sea

MAGNETIC +
POLE, 1960

ANTARCTIC EXPEDITIONS 1911–1958

Filchner (1911–1912)

Byrd (1929)

Mawson (1929–1930)

Mawson (1930–1931)

Ellsworth (1935)

Graham Land Expedition (1934–1937)

British Commonwealth TransAntarctic
Expedition (1957–1958)

⊗ International Expedition Bases 1956–1958

Ice shelves

Permanent sea ice

military operation than the pioneering attempts of earlier explorers. They covered the 2,158 miles (3,500 km) between November and March.

Their trek included a stopover at the Amundsen-Scott base, where for five days Fuchs's team enjoyed hot showers and a few movies. Throughout their trek they took soundings which showed that the ice was up to 9,000 feet (2,700 m) thick, and that entire mountain ranges lay buried beneath the ice cap.

SET INDEX